T0149355

A Christian's
JOURNEY

A Christian's
JOURNEY

PASTOR LERONE DINNALL

A CHRISTIAN'S JOURNEY

Scripture quotations from the Holy Bible, King James Version (Authorized Version). First published in 1611. Quoted from the KJV Classic Reference Bible.

iUniverse books may be ordered through booksellers or by contacting:

iUniverse
1663 Liberty Drive
Bloomington, IN 47403
www.iuniverse.com
1-800-Authors (1-800-288-4677)

ISBN: 978-1-5320-7978-8 (sc)
ISBN: 978-1-5320-7979-5 (e)

Print information available on the last page.

iUniverse rev. date: 08/06/2019

TABLE OF CONTENTS

A Tribute vii

Introduction... ix

Opening Scripture... xv

Mindset xvii

Break Into Trust For God... 1

The Mystery of Being Empty.. 12

Receiving The Spirit of Obedience 16

The Lord Will Provide 24

Mountains; Valleys; Storms and Seas; Fire and Water; The
Different Challenges of A Christian's Journey 40

Spend Your Time Seeking To Get To That Better Home.......... 56

The Walls of Difficulties... 65

Nothing Is Wrong If We Cry or Become Frustrated
During The Test; Our Main Job Is To Finish The Test... 69

Stopping The CRY!.. 77

Let Us Take A Closer Look.. 85

The King's Wine 91

The Difference Between Giving up to That of Letting Go.......... 100

The Giving That Brings Forth God's Release................................ 106
Why Does God's Best, Appears To Be My Worse?..................... 113
A Successful Ministry 123
The Levels of Faith..134

Closing Scripture 157
Conclusion...159

A Tribute

"To The Eternal Spirit of Intelligence, To God Be All Glory, Honor and Praise from Beginning to Ending and from Everlasting to Eternity, My Soul Must Worship God".

"A Special Tribute to all Saints that are True to their purpose for God".

INTRODUCTION

LET ALL GLORY, HONOR and Praise Be Directed to The God of The Universe, Jesus Christ The Lamb of God. I count myself as living a Dream that God Has Permitted for me to live, realizing that when The Lord First Asked me to Build an Altar for His Glory, I had no expectation that His Ministry would have found me in this Position to become an Author, to speak and to inspire God's People who are set to Inherit God's Kingdom.

If we could identify the Spiritual sequence in which The Lord is Permitting these Books to be Released, we would have identified that the First Book with the Title God Steps In seeks to establish the Foundation Materials that are needed for every true Child of God to Know in order to use to ensure that they have A Personal Relationship with The Father that will be able to stand every passing storms of life. The Second Book with the Title Rebuild Your Spiritual Wall is aimed to allow those who are destined for The Kingdom of God to understand that if we are going to make it to the point of which The Trumpet of The Lord Sounds, we must be ever determine to understand that The Spiritual Walls of each Believer must be made firm and maintained in order for God's Covenant of Peace to be Furnished upon our lives and the lives of our generation to follow in our footsteps. This third Book with the Title A Christian's Journey will educate each Believer in a personal way, which will see each Testimony of this Book act as a Spiritual Guideline to make us aware of The Journey that must be travelled with patience and with a conscious mind, to know that it is not going to be easy, but in order to receive Heaven, this Christian's Journey is a Must.

Within the contents of this Book I needed to ensure that I made some difference to how this Book will be used by the Readers, therefore as usual, beginning from the first Book to this third Book there are Prayers within this Book, also I implemented sections in this Book that the Readers are able to personalize their own copy of this Book to answer Questions which are asked by the Topics that are being read. I need My Readers to have a unique touch with their Book while reading, that will enable the Readers to become comfortable, just as how we are comfortable reading our Bibles and able to do little jotting of Revelations on the sides of our Bibles, thus it will be seen at the ending of this Book that there is a section called The Personal Touch of Revelations from God, this was designed for the benefit of My Readers.

A Christian's Journey begins with the first Chapter seeking to challenge the minds of God's People, to allow for us to understand that there is a Physical life and also a Spiritual life that is occupying a believer's body at the same time. This Chapter will demonstrate to God's People that if we are leaning too much on the Physical manifestation of life, then The Spiritual Birth of God's Unbelievable Miracles will never be experienced by a Believer who is seeking to walk the road of this Christian's Journey. Thus within this Chapter a Believer will be Inspired in the way of The Spirit's Direction to Manifest the Secret path for a believer to break from the Physical Mind to be born in The Spiritual Mind.

There are times in our lives as Christians that we just cannot understand the Movements of The Spirit of God within our lives, we know for certain that we are Serving God and The Relationship is intact, but there are times on this Journey we are left to wonder what is happening in a time and cycle of our lives. The second Chapter of this Book will reveal through Visions that I've Received from God of what God is Doing in the times of our lives that we are in a position of being empty, and also what we as Children of God should be doing when these times does occur in our lives.

It is found that many Christians have been disciplined to go to Church and to participate in the activities of a Church, but when Church is over, we still have not been born to understand Who is our Master, because after Church has ended, it now becomes the norm to go back and to do that which God Required of us not to Do. This evidence shows that we have not yet Received The Spirit of Obedience that will Cause, Force and Demand The Living Conscience of The Spirit of God to thus Dictate our actions for God's Purpose in our lives.

Moving on through this Book we will be greeted with a personal Message of mine that brings tears to my eyes every time I pick up this Message to read. This Message is known as The Lord Will Provide. I Received The Anointing to write this Message based on a personal experience I had with a customer. The Lord Allowed the pain of this experience to become The Anointed Birth for many that will be in a position like this to know that through this experience, The Lord Will Bring Forth A New Relationship with His Children to Understand that He Never Fails The Job of Providing for His Children, He Never failed in the Past, it will not be experienced in the Present, therefore the Future looks bright for all those who will put their Trust in The Hands of The Heavenly Father, because God Will Provide.

Have we ever noticed in the past or present that many that have instructed people to come to Christ, their message was focused to tell others that all will be well if they surrender their lives to God. By doing this it created a picture in the minds of new believers to think that once they have been Baptized, then they are immediately going to walk on streets of gold without the Trial of Being A Christian. Let us think for a minute, I know we think that we are doing a good job by advising new believers in this format, and at whatever cost we must seek to lead others to Christ, but we should desire to Ask God to Impart on us The

Spirit of Discernment to identify that if we continue the Message of all will be Well; then it will be Reveal through The Voice and Spirit of God that we are in fact Deceiving others by painting a picture which is a lie. I've found out that the best method is The Truth, after we have spoken The Truth to someone who is desiring to give their lives over to God, then that person will forever Respect such a person whether they decide to surrender their lives over to God or not. The Truth is The Truth, and nothing can change The Truth. Therefore in the fifth Chapter of this Book, The Truth about a Christian's Journey is what is expressed. After reading about The Truth, those who are determined to continue on this Journey will Manifest The Material that God is Searching for to Populate His Kingdom.

There are many people that have spent years in a job that have not brought forth a sense of satisfaction, many have spent years in Relationship that is ugly, many have burden themselves in companies and family members that have not yielded any fruits, many are currently in a Church and is yet to Experience The Touch that only God Can Give; and to all this I will Advise my Readers that this is only Vanity. Our lives is being wasted away on things that is only active for the day, and afterwards there is absolutely no more value of that which we've worked so hard to accomplish in this life, again I say this is Vanity. Chapter six of this Book will refresh a Child of God's mind to be focused on that which is really Important in this life, which is to ensure that we enter The Gate of God's Kingdom. Everything else is Vanity, why waste all our Time, Energy and Recourses on that which will and must fade away one day. It just doesn't make sense.

Chapter seven speaks about the Spiritual Prison that a Believer will encounter if we have not identified within ourselves the use of The Spiritual Key that is only available by doing that which God Requires for His People to Fulfill.

Chapters eight and nine encourages a Believer to Cry out to God and keep crying, because there is a Vessel in Heaven that captures our tears and when that Vessel is Full, it Will and Must Activate The Purpose of God upon the lives of those who have Positioned themselves to Cry out to God for their Deliverance.

There are times in our lives as Christians that we've got to decide that we are going to take inventory of our Christian walk; because if we will not see the importance of making sure that we are on The Foundation, then there will be a day that will decide for us if we were on The Foundation. The unfortunate thing about that day is that we won't be able to change or to fix anything, therefore, if we cannot identify the faults in our walk now, then that day when all is called to The Judgement will leave us on the Wrong side of God's Mercy. Chapters ten and eleven will demonstrate the type of actions a Child of God Must take to be and remain a Vessel of Honor unto God.

Chapter twelve will no doubt challenge the minds of God's Chosen Inheritance, to let us Identify The True Power when we move and abide within The Wave of The Spirit of God for our lives. It must be born in our understanding to know that God's Spirit Moves within our lives to Create Clean Sacrifice that will force God's Will to Be Done. At times when God's Spirit is Moving which causes us to lose some possessions, hence we should not be troubled by this because everything that is lost is a material that was not needed for the full manifestation of God's Glory within our lives.

There is a secret that has been lost to this world, and that secret it to know how to give to God that will force The God of The Universe to Release Favors upon the lives of those who have released to God in the fashion in which God Desires. Chapter Thirteen of this Book will seek to Educate God's People to Break out of the custom of which this world seeks to offer kindness, that prevents The Movement of God's Favor to be Released.

Chapter Fourteen is a live Testimony that every Child of God Have Asked God in their Prayers. This Chapter will bring forth a sense of comfort to the lives of Christians that are on this Journey, by allowing us to understand that everything that we have experienced being bad on this Journey will one day Manufacture Everything Good in God's Kingdom. We will identify that in order to Inherit Eternal life, that means that the Physical life and ambitions has to die. Thus resulting in us not having a life that is of physical desires to live in this life.

When I was Called by God to Build an Altar for The Name of Jesus Christ, the first thing that came to my mind was: How was I going to do this for God? My Investigation brought me to write about this Message in the Fifteen Chapter called A Successful Ministry. I Asked The Lord to Lead me in the right path to identify through His Words, that I would not only Start the Altar but to Build and Maintain A Spiritual Building that will Stand every Storms, Test, Powers, Demonic Influence and also the forces of evil altars. The Lord Revealed to me through this Message The Foundation of Any Successful Ministry. The Lord Identify that if The Ministry is being Built on Him, of which His Name Is Jesus Christ, then there is no way that Ministry Can Fail. St Matthew Chapter 16:18. A part of this Verse Says:

"UPON THIS ROCK I WILL BUILD MY CHURCH, AND THE GATES OF HELL SHALL NOT PREVAIL AGAINST IT".

The Final Message of this Book is Called The Levels of Faith, there is currently many Christians that read about Faith but are still confused has to what Faith Is. This Final Message will Graduate The Spirit Man in every believer to thus climb up towards the continual higher Level of Faith in God which does exist. Jesus Christ Said: "GREATER WORKS THAN THESE WHICH I HAVE DONE SHALL YOU BE ABLE TO DO, BECAUSE I GO TO MY FATHER". We are The Greater Works, It's time to Manifest The Greater Works In The Mighty Name of Jesus Christ.

Before The Lord Created The Burning for me to Release these Messages in a Book, I was always writing these Messages and just gave them away to as many that has need to receive of an Inspiring Word that God Had Caused me to write. To God Be The Glory, I'm Happy that these Books with these Messages can reach the lives of many that are to be Saved through The Mighty Saving Name of Jesus Christ. The Eternal Spirit of God Goes with the words of this Book, that whoever comes in contact with this Book, they will encounter The Fresh Anointing that God Has Released through these words.

To The Eternal Father, The Only Unlimited Mind of The Universe, Jesus Christ The Lamb of God, to Him Be All Glory, Honor and Praise, Amen.

OPENING SCRIPTURE

EXODUS CHAPTER 14:13-31.

"And Moses said unto the people, Fear ye not, stand still, and see the Salvation of The Lord, which He Will Shew to you to day: for the Egyptians whom ye have seen to day, ye shall see them again no more for ever. The Lord Shall Fight for you, and ye shall hold your peace. And The Lord Said unto Moses, Wherefore criest thou unto Me? Speak unto the children of Israel, that they go forward: But lift thou up thy rod, and stretch out thine hand over the sea, and divide it: and the children of Israel shall go on dry ground through the midst of the sea. And I, behold, I Will harden the hearts of the Egyptians, and they shall follow them: and I Will get Me honour upon Pharaoh, and upon all his host, upon his chariots, and upon his horsemen. And the Egyptians shall know that I Am The Lord, when I have gotten me honour upon Pharaoh, upon his chariots, and upon his horsemen. And The Angel of God, which went before the camp of Israel, removed and went behind them; and the pillar of the cloud went from before their face, and stood behind them: And it came between the camp of the Egyptians and the camp of Israel; and it was a cloud and darkness to them, but it gave light by night to these: so that the one came not near the other all the night.

And Moses stretch out his hand over the sea; and The Lord Caused the sea to go back by a strong east wind all that night, and made the sea dry land, and the waters were divided. And the children of Israel went into the midst of the sea upon the dry ground: and the waters were a wall unto them on their right hand, and on their left. And the Egyptians pursued, and went in after them to the midst of the sea, even all Pharaoh's horses, his chariots, and his horsemen. And it came to pass, that in the morning watch The Lord Looked unto the host of the Egyptians through the pillar of fire and of the cloud, and Troubled the host of the Egyptians, and Took off their chariot wheels, that they drave them heavily: so that the Egyptians said, Let us flee from the face of Israel; for The Lord Fighteth for them against the Egyptians. And The Lord Said unto Moses, Stretch out thine hand over the sea, that the waters may come again upon the Egyptians, upon their chariots, and upon their horsemen.

And Moses Stretch forth his hand over the sea, and the sea returned to his strength when the morning appeared; and the Egyptians fled against it; and The Lord Overthrew the Egyptians in the midst of the sea. And the waters returned, and covered the chariots, and the horsemen, and all the host of Pharaoh that came into the sea after them; there remained not so much as one of them. But the children of Israel walked upon dry land in the midst of the sea; and the waters were a wall unto them on their right hand, and on their left. Thus The Lord Saved Israel that day out of the hand of the Egyptians; and Israel saw the Egyptians dead upon the sea shore. And Israel saw that great work which The Lord Did upon the Egyptians: and the people feared The Lord, and believed The Lord, and His Servant Moses".

MINDSET

- At The Cross road of Decision, make certain to listen to The Soul, because the Soul still has a resemblance of God's Will Being Done.

- The Spirit of God Is A Wave, It's Unpredictable, It's Moves in Ways that Confuses the Intelligence of Man.

- Think! Those who follows the path and design of this life for years, where are they now? If you can find them; Do they have The Peace of God?

- Think! Those who have Sacrificed the pleasures of this life for The Cross of Jesus Christ, when we do find them, it is echoed in our spirits that it is well, because those persons have found The Rest for their Souls.

- It may become a lonely road on the Narrow path, but remember, any Journey that includes The Presence of God is more than worth all lifetimes of the pleasures of this life.

- Get off the fast lane of life, the End will be Sudden and it does not have a Warning Light!

- The Eternal Spirit of God Wasn't Move to Change the Direction and Pathway of Jesus Christ when He Cried for The Cup of death to be moved. Therefore, God Will Not Be Interested in any excuse that prevents us from walking on the path of The Christian's Journey.

- Let our Souls repeat this Prayer: Lord Jesus Christ, Let Your Will Be Done in my life, Amen.

BREAK INTO TRUST
FOR GOD

Message # 91

Date Started February 18, 2018

Date Finalized February 20, 2018.

IT IS CONVENIENT THAT this Message # 91 begins with this Scripture: Psalms 91.

"HE THAT DWELLETH IN THE SECRET PLACE OF THE MOST HIGH SHALL ABIDE UNDER THE SHADOW OF THE ALMIGHTY. I WILL SAY OF THE LORD, HE IS MY REFUGE AND MY FORTRESS: MY GOD; IN HIM WILL I TRUST. SURELY HE SHALL DELIVER THEE FROM THE SNARE OF THE FOWLER, AND FROM THE NOISOME PESTILENCE. HE SHALL COVER THEE WITH HIS FEATHERS, AND UNDER HIS WINGS SHALT THOU TRUST: HIS TRUTH SHALL BE THY SHIELD AND BUCKLER. THOU SHALT NOT BE AFRAID FOR THE TERROR BY NIGHT; NOR FOR THE ARROW THAT FLIETH BY DAY; NOR FOR THE PESTILENCE THAT WALKETH IN DARKNESS; NOR FOR THE DESTRUCTION THAT WASTETH AT NOONDAY.

A THOUSAND SHALL FALL AT THY SIDE, AND TEN THOUSAND AT THY RIGHT HAND; BUT IT SHALL NOT COME NIGH THEE. ONLY WITH THINE EYES SHALT THOU BEHOLD AND SEE THE REWARD OF THE WICKED. BECAUSE THOU HAST MADE THE LORD, WHICH IS MY REFUGE, EVEN THE MOST HIGH, THY HABITATION; THERE SHALL NO EVIL BEFALL THEE, NEITHER SHALL ANY PLAGUE COME NIGH THY DWELLING. FOR HE SHALL GIVE HIS ANGELS CHARGE OVER THEE, TO KEEP THEE IN ALL THY WAYS. THEY SHALL BEAR THEE UP IN THEIR HANDS, LEST THOU DASH THY FOOT AGAINST A STONE.

THOU SHALT TREAD UPON THE LION AND ADDER: THE YOUNG LION AND DRAGON SHALT THOU TRAMPLE UNDER FEET. BECAUSE HE HATH SET HIS LOVE UPON ME, THEREFORE WILL I DELIVER HIM: I WILL SET HIM ON HIGH, BECAUSE HE HATH KNOWN MY NAME. HE SHALL CALL UPON ME, AND I WILL ANSWER HIM: I WILL BE WITH HIM IN TROUBLE; I WILL DELIVER HIM, AND HONOUR HIM. WITH LONG LIFE WILL I SATISFY HIM, AND SHEW HIM MY SALVATION".

Wonderful Councilor, Mighty God, Everlasting Father, Prince of Peace, Saviour of Mankind, Jesus Christ The Lamb of God. I Greet All My Fathers Children in The Name of Jesus Christ our Soon Coming King. Glad am I to be in this Position to speak again to God's People through the Writing of Inspired Messages. There are a lot of us, even Christians, that believe that we Trust God, and we even speak that word of Trust out of our mouth by Testifying to Acknowledge that we Trust God. Now, I am not here to beat on anyone that is exercising their rights to create a Belief Environment of Trust for God; because speaking things into being is exactly what God Need for us to Practice. But there will come a time that just speaking the Words to exercise our Faith is just not good enough nor is it sufficient, because it is a Fact every Trust for God will be Tested; thus allowing those of us who proclaim the word Trust for God to now become of the Attitude and the Mind frame that we are now Born into Trust for God and His Word.

The word Trust for God and His Word cannot be Separated from the words Relationship with God, because every Child of God that Declares the word Trust in God and for God, will soon to discover that there is A Spirit of Truth to Discern, to Burn, and to Try the Now Active Relationship that A Child of God Has Declared that they have with The Father Above.

If we could remember the seven sons of Sceva who was in fact the chief of the Priest, his sons saw Paul casting out devils in The Name of Jesus Christ and thought to themselves that we can do the same thing as well, because we are sons of the Chief Priest; The Bible Declares that they tried to do the same thing that Paul had done, then soon discovered that the Demons that was in the individual spoke to them and asked them in summary:

"WHERE IS YOUR TRUST FOR GOD, WHERE IS YOUR RELATIONSHIP WITH GOD; BECAUSE, PAUL I KNOW; JESUS I KNOW; BUT WHO ARE YE"!

The Demons Beat and Wounded these young men that they ran out of the house naked. This Story can be read for more understanding in The Book of Acts 19:11-20.

Truth be told, it is going to take a while for A Child of God to now find themselves in A Position that they have now Broken the Glass of Separation that have separated themselves from The Complete Divine Relationship of Trust that they must now be Born into, to realize the path of Divine Blessings from The Father Above.

Break Into Trust for God. Question: How can A Christian Break into Trust for God? _____.

The number one answer I can give to Christians is to have a Sure Diet for God, in that we have found ourselves to Become Disciplined to Follow The Diet of Spiritual Maturity; this however is going to require The Spirit of Patience, it is not an overnight fix; nor can it be established for those who are not Determined to Follow The Ways of The Lord. Trust for God is 100% Personal; this means that even if we are Married and our Husband and Wife are Pastors, that individual cannot Trust God for you; Breaking into Trust comes from your Personal Relationship that you have Developed with God.

Whenever our Test Comes, who is the person that faces that

Test? _____. Truth; is it not the person that is Experiencing the Test! Even though we may ask our Husband and Wife who is in The Office of A Pastor to Pray, that prayer can only do so much, to now bring that person that is in the Process of their Test to Elevate their Belief in God, that will now cause their own Belief to Brake the Glass of Separation of Trust, that Allows that Believer to be Born in The Relationship of Trust, that because they Trust God and now Know about God; whatever they are Facing truly have no Power to hurt them because The Spirit of Trust for God Is Completely and Divinely Fixed in them, Around them, and for their Entire life and the life of their Generations to follow.

The Servant Daniel gave us a Prime Example of what it means to Truly Trust In God. In The Book of Daniel Chapter 6. In Summary it is Explained that Daniel had in him An Excellent Spirit, and because of The Excellent Spirit that God Has Given to Daniel, this means that Daniel was now Promoted in High Authority; this was not pleasing in the eyes of all the other servants, therefore, they devised a plan to the effect that this plan would have succeeded to get rid of Daniel and his God, along with his Practices and Customs. The servants came to the king under the disguise of wanting to Honour the king for a period of time, therefore, they asked the king to sign a Decree which cannot be altered; and the Decree was made against Daniel and The Relationship that Daniel Possessed with his God. Now there is a part of The Scripture I would like to bring to Light for My Readers; in Verse 10. The Bible Declared:

"NOW WHEN DANIEL KNEW THAT THE WRITING WAS SIGNED, HE WENT INTO HIS HOUSE; AND HIS WINDOWS BEING OPEN IN HIS CHAMBER TOWARDS JERUSALEM, HE KNEELED UPON HIS KNEES THREE TIMES A DAY, AND PRAYED, AND GAVE THANKS BEFORE HIS GOD, AS HE DID AFORETIME".

The Bible Said that Daniel Knew that the writing that was to sentence him to Death was signed; he knew! After knowing what was to come if he did not break his Relationship with God; if he did not Break his Trust for God; Daniel now decided that The Relationship and Trust that he has Developed with God is one than needed to be Kept and Nourished, and no writings of Laws that was signed by the king himself was not going to prevent him from Losing The Connection that he has with God. Daniel Knew, he went to his home knowing that the enemies was watching every step that he makes; he decided that he was going to make it easy for them. The Bible Said that Daniel had is windows open as he was accustomed to do, he went on his knees to Pray, to keep The Relationship, to keep The Trust that he has Developed with His God, not even wondering about what the enemies would do, he had an Appointment with His Father that no King, no President, and no Prince was going to stop, because Daniel would have Developed his Personal Relationship with God that sees himself breaking every glass of Trust that separated himself from God. Now if that which Daniel did, if this does not spell the word CONFIDENCE FOR GOD, then I cannot explain what else it was.

Breaking Into Trust For God; this will allow each Servant of God to Become of The Attitude and Spirit of Confidence. We will now Walk Confident, we will now Speak Confident, we will Behave ourselves in a Confident Manner, and also we will Smell Confident. Whenever it is that we enter a room that is of some other spirits, the very moment we walk through the Doors of that room, that which is Dispelled from us is The Spirit of Confidence which Births The Revelation of The Light of God to any conditions that seeks to Trap and Entangle the life of those who are Oppressed. The Spirit of God in us would have now Spring Forth an Odor of Sweet Godly Scent, that whosoever smells and comes in contact with such a Person that is Serving God with A Relationship and Trust for God, that person would have been Blessed by the very Presence of Any Child of God that simply walks in the Pathway and Atmosphere that they are in.

Back to The Story of Daniel: The Bible Said that Daniel went on his knees and gave God Thanks.

REALLY!

REALLY!

First The Bible Mentioned that Daniel knew that the writing was signed for him to be put to death if he Kept The Relationship and Trust that he have Developed with God; and the first thing to come

5

in the Mind of Daniel when he went down on his knees to pray was to Give God Thanks. WOW! I can just imagine the Prayer that was made to God.

"LORD GOD OF ABRAHAM, THE GOD OF ISAAC AND THE GOD OF ISRAEL; I COME BEFORE YOU THIS DAY TO GIVE YOU THANKS; ALTHOUGH LORD, THIS IS THE DAY APPOINTED FOR ME TO DIE, BECAUSE I AM KNOWLEDGEABLE OF WHAT IS TO COME, BUT IN SPITE OF ALL THIS LORD, I GIVE YOU THANKS; LORD I'M GOING TO BE CAST IN THE LION'S DEN, BUT I GIVE YOU THANKS; LORD, THE KING WHO I THOUGHT WAS MY GOOD FRIEND HAS SIGNED THE WRITINGS FOR ME TO DIE IF I PRAY UNTO MY GOD, AND FOR THIS LORD, I GIVE YOU THANKS.

LORD, I THANK YOU FOR THIS DAY OF MISERY; LORD I THANK YOU FOR WHAT THE ENEMIES THINKS THAT THEY CAN DO TO ME; LORD I THANK YOU FOR THE RELATIONSHIP AND THE TRUST THAT I HAVE IN YOU, THAT EVEN IF YOU WILL ALLOW FOR ME TO DIE AT THE HANDS OF MY ENEMIES, LORD I GIVE YOU THANKS. LORD I THANK YOU FOR WHAT I'VE EXPERIENCED IN THE PAST; LORD I THANK YOU FOR WHAT I'M EXPERIENCING NOW; AND LORD I THANK YOU FOR WHAT I'M ABOUT TO EXPERIENCE IN THE FUTURE; LORD I GIVE YOU THANKS. THANK YOU LORD BECAUSE EVERYTHING IS ALREADY IN YOUR HANDS. I WILL END MY PRAYER BY SAYING THANK YOU LORD, THANK YOU LORD, THANK YOU LORD, AMEN".

How many of us that are Serving The Living God, would have had an Appetite or A Spirit of Peace to that effect, that would have seen ourselves entering the Sure End of our lives, and even if we Prayed, would The Prayer be Geared to make certain that this is A Prayer of Thanksgiving unto God? How Many of us!

Now we've realized that there are Levels in The Relationship and Trust for God; Levels that we have not even started to Scratch the surface of that type of Anointing that Brings forth A Unique Relationship of Trust with The God of The Universe. Many of us, Truth be told, even if we found ourselves to go before God in Prayer, being of the knowledge that death is Eminent, it is a Fact, The Prayer would not be A Prayer to Give God Thanks. The rest of The Story in The Book of Daniel Chapter 6. Proved that once we are A Child of The King, and it is certain that we have Broken the Glass of Trust for God, which brings forth The True Divine Relationship with God. Then it is Certain, as it was Proven to Daniel and all the people of that time, Kings, Presidents, Princes; it doesn't matter who it is; it will be Proven again and again that God Regards Relationship that Springs forth Trust from His People.

Relationship that brings forth Trust will Birth The Revelation of The Divine Intimate God to now Step off His Throne without Leaving His Throne, to now Step into the Rules and the Laws that was Set to Destroy Those Children that have Manifested A Great Trust for God through Relationship.

This type of Deliverance was also Experienced in Chapter 3 of The Book Daniel. When God Stepped Into the Councils of that which man had put together to Oppress and put in Bondage the lives of God's Chosen People who Trust in Him. There are three Verses in Chapter 3. That I would like My Readers to get the Full understanding of. Verse 16-18.

"SHADRACH, MESHACH, AND ABEDNEGO, ANSWERED AND SAID TO THE KING, O NEBUCHADNEZZAR, WE ARE NOT CAREFUL TO ANSWER THEE IN THIS MATTER. IF IT BE SO, OUR GOD WHOM WE SERVE IS ABLE TO DELIVER US FROM THE BURNING FIERY FURNACE, AND HE WILL DELIVER US OUT OF THINE HAND, O KING. BUT IF NOT, BE IT KNOWN UNTO THEE, O KING, THAT WE WILL NOT SERVE THY GODS, NOR WORSHIP THE GOLDEN IMAGE WHICH THOU HAST SET UP".

Again we Read, we Hear and Feel The Spirit of Confidence within the lives of three of God's Servants. In many ways it can be said that these three young men was in fact Disrespectful to the king; but when your Serving God, and you know that you know that you KNOW, that there is in Fact an Active Relationship with The Father, there is no amount of Threats and laws that is signed that will Shut Up A Child of God's Anointing from Declaring who Exactly their God is to them.

Break Into Trust For God; there was a time in my life, when The Man of God, Bishop Austin Whitfield was still alive. He Saw the Importance of me establishing A Relationship with God and for God, in that he would always Encourage and Demand for me to spend as much time that I can spend in The Words of God to Develop My Relationship with God. Bishop Whitfield would often DEMAND for me to spend more time coming to Church when he saw that work was now occupying most of my time. Bishop would DEMAND from me being a young Minister, to be more a part of The Fasting Services. Bishop Whitfield made sure that I spent Two years straight, to be in Prayer Meetings at Church, and Prayer Meeting began at 6AM sharp every morning except for Wednesdays, Fridays and Sundays, which was Fasting days and general Worship days.

Bishop Whitfield even made sure that I got Married to the person that he handpicked to be My Wife before he went to Rest. This was how important The Man of God Identified that there must be A Relationship of Trust for God Developed in My Life. 70% of what Bishop Whitfield was preparing me for, I had No Clue. It's now that he has pass away, I discovered that even though he's gone to Rest and I will not see him again until Time has come to an end; I also discovered that all he has Forced me to Learn from coming to Church, going to conduct Prayer Meetings, going to conduct Fasting Meetings, Teaching Sunday School; being the Young People's President for over ten years; I discovered that all that he has taught me to know about God and His Word and Work, it remains with me; Bishop Austin Whitfield is gone to Rest, but His Work that he has Invested in me Lives on still.

I made mention of this Experience with The Man of God to allow My Readers to understand that there is no way A Child of God Can Break Into Trust For God, unless that Servant now decides that they are going to do all that is required of them to do to know about God. A Child of God has to know the Importance of why Prayer is Necessary to their Development of Trust for God. A Child of God needs to know why the Prayer of Thanksgiving is of utmost importance to themselves and for The Relationship that they have

Developed with God. A Child of God have to Discover that in their Prayers to God, there must be a part in the Prayer that we Ask God to Forgive us of our Sins, before we even enter into discussion with God for what we need for God to do for us, this would now be the Prayer of Request. Because if sin remains in the life of A Child of God, how will we receive that which we need from God, seeing that everything we Ask God for, the first thing that God will first See is the Unconfessed Sins. This is called Roadblocks in our Prayers. A Child of God needs to understand that in their Prayers, there must be a part that we have separated to make sure that we Pray for others; it is called The Prayer of Brotherly Love. How can we love God and not Love others that are Serving God like yourself and also those who have not yet Tasted that The Lord Is GOOD.

That's it for Prayer. Moving on; A Child of God must Train themselves to be a part of Fasting and Fasting Services. I gave Commands to all those who are a part of The Assembly that I am responsible for, especially those who work for a living; I told them to make certain that there is not one month that will pass that they have not done at least one day of Fasting within that one month; this should be done for their own Personal Development and Relationship with God. That's how Important Fasting is. In a Nut Shell, those Christians who don't Pray a lot, and don't find the time to Fast for their Personal Development in God; they don't Read The Words of God has they should; they don't come to Church Regularly. I told The Church Members that this is in Fact a Recipe for Disaster, there is no way that such A Child of God can remain Saved.

We are Freely Given Saving Grace not to stop from Maintaining that Faith of Salvation, but rather, that which God Has Entrust us with, Requires A Daily Purposeful Maintenance. This Physical life also Teaches us this Fact; if we buy a New Car, the first thing that we would be recommended to do for that Car even before we leave the Car Mart, is to make certain that within a specific time, to perform the Servicing of the Vehicle that would be necessary, because the Vehicle will require Maintenance.

For those of us who are Married, we all know by now that the easiest part of the Marriage was the day we had our Ceremony and Vowed to God by saying I DO. After that day, it Requires A Continual Meaningful Maintenance Every Day with The Help of God to Allow that Marriage to Stay Connected. If we don't work on our Marriage Daily, then it is certain we have no one to blame but ourselves, the Marriage Will Die. That's the Rule for the Physical, so it is also the Rule for The Spiritual. No Spiritual Work to Maintain our Relationship with God, this means no Meaningful Relationship, therefore, We will never Break forth to Truly Trust In God. Trust will only remain a word that we speak forth in Testimony and in Songs and in Reading, we will never Experience it for ourselves.

Breaking Into Trust For God; the beginning of this experience starts with A Child of God's Diet for God; after A Child of Starts and begin to Maintain that Diet, then The Lord Will Now Say:

"IT IS NOW TIME FOR ME TO BREAK MY SERVANT COMPLETELY FROM THE PHYSICAL MIND TO THAT OF THE SPIRITUAL MIND".

And when this Time in our lives have Started; for those who are viewing Physically, it will be expressed to be the worse time in that Child of God life; because to Break from the Physical, The Spirit of God now has to Train us to Break from Physical, and the Tool God Uses to Train is Fire. For those who have Tasted of The Spiritual Experience, they would have understood that, that which A Child of God is now Experiencing, is in Fact The Process of Transformation from Physical to Spiritual.

A lot of things that we think we need in this life for our Christian's Journey, when God Begins to Train, we would have discovered that the only Thing that God Requires from us, is only our Souls. Our Money, God Don't Need that for Transformation; God Don't Need our Car, No, not our Homes; the Job is not a Requirement; our Husbands and Wives will also require their Personal Transformation. Diplomas, Degrees and Certificates; all these are Burnt up in the Process of God's Transformation. During the period of Time of God Doing the Work of Transformation; it's going to be the most Dark and Lonely road that person ever Travels on. But as long as we are certain that we are in the Process of Transformation from Physical to Spiritual, then we are certain that there is A Brighter Light at the end of the Journey, which will bring us into Complete Trust for God.

From The Ministry of The Church of Jesus Christ Fellowship Savannah Cross Ltd. I Hope this Message would have help a least one person, in The Name of Jesus Christ I Pray. Continue to Pray for this Ministry. From Pastor Lerone Dinnall.

BREAK INTO GOD'S TRUST.

THE MYSTERY OF BEING EMPTY

Message # 77   **Date Started August 2, 2017**
                          Date Finalized August 2, 2017.

1 KINGS CHAPTER 17:1-6.

"AND ELIJAH THE TISBITE, WHO WAS OF THE INHABITANTS OF GILEAD, SAID UNTO AHAB, AS THE LORD GOD OF ISRAEL LIVETH, BEFORE WHOM I STAND, THERE SHALL NOT BE DEW NOR RAIN THESE YEARS, BUT ACCORDING TO MY WORD. AND THE WORD OF THE LORD CAME UNTO HIM, SAYING, GET THEE HENCE, AND TURN THEE EASTWARD, AND HIDE THYSELF BY THE BROOK CHERITH, THAT IS BEFORE JORDAN. AND IT SHALL BE, THAT THOU SHALT DRINK OF THE BROOK; AND I HAVE COMMANDED THE RAVENS TO FEED THEE THERE. SO HE WENT AND DID ACCORDING UNTO THE WORD OF THE LORD: FOR HE WENT AND DWELT BY THE BROOK CHERITH, THAT IS BEFORE JORDAN. AND THE RAVENS BROUGHT HIM BREAD AND FLESH IN THE EVENING; AND HE DRANK OF THE BROOK".

I Give Honour and Praise to The Almighty Father, The Prince of Peace; The Saviour of Mankind, Jesus Christ, The Lamb of God. Privileged and Honored am I to be writing another Inspiring Message. Let's get to it. The Topic says: "THE MYSTERY OF BEING EMPTY". I got this Topic by means of A Vision in the Early Morning of Sleep, and I got up immediately to begin writing what was Revealed to me by The Voice of The Lord.

Now The Lord Reveals that for those who have acquired a level in Him and is actually walking in that same Level of Righteousness and Holiness before God; it is to be compared to that of The Foundation of God's Word that Is Walking and Talking, Living and Continue to Be What God would have for us to Be; Demonstrating to Ourselves, the World and to God that we are indeed The Temple of The Living God. Now for this Person that have found the Discipline to be of The Characteristics of God; such a person has nothing to be afraid of, because The God of The Universe Fills Every Gap.

The Lord Reveals that the problem He Has with Saints is the desires that we have attained to be SELF-SUFFICIENT, without realizing the clear Fact that once we have elevated to become The Walking Righteousness and Holiness for The Lord, then it would have been established that we are not the responsibility of our own Will and Desires, but now have become the full Responsibility of God Almighty. It is with this clear evidence that The Lord Brought forth this Topic.

While it is the Attitude and the Character of a person or Child of God that is not enduring the Process of becoming Born Again to go forth and to fend for themselves that which they desire and require for their daily sustenance, and to even make provisions in numerous quantity to ensure that their future doesn't catch them off guard. The Lord Reveals that, for a person to be of this Mindset, it explains and brings to Manifestation that such a person have not yet Elevated to the Level to Understand that The Foundation of God Stands Forever; therefore meaning that if A Child of God is The True Foundation of The Word of God, then that Child of God need not to Worry, Wonder, be Concern about anything that is taking place in the outside World because that which is taking place can never and will never even come close to that person who have found The Foundation of God's Word to be their ROCK.

The Lord Reveals that there is a constant Struggle for those who are Children of God, that have not yet FULLY SURRENDERED TO HIS WILL; in that the Physical Will continues to hold on to the Physical elements of that which they can see and feel. And by doing this, this Child of God remains in the Natural with the desires to still remain in the Natural and be able to receive of The Divine Blessings of The Spiritual; of which both cannot Mix.

The Lord Reveals that the Natural bears the evidence of the powers of gods, meaning Idols, of which it is Limited, Vain and only last for a Time and a Season. On the other hand, that which is Spiritual is for Eternity, meaning that those who will Grasp the importance of receiving The Fullness of that which is Spiritual, would not only have received it for their lifetime, but will Cement The Divine Blessing for all Lifetime, all Generations throughout all the time of Life, and then after to Inherit The Kingdom of God; this meaning that each Surrender we give unto God to Attain The Fullness of The Spiritual, will manifest not only for ourselves, but will be Established also for our Children The Revelations of Divine Interventions.

Being and becoming Empty does not mean that we are going to sit aside and say to ourselves that The Lord Will Provide without any movement by ourselves; no that's not what The Lord is Revealing. Rather, The Lord Is Revealing that there are times He Create the Environment to facilitate small portions, CALLED THE ALONE TIME, that He Can Now Fill the Gap of that which remains, and it is found in the period or Process of having Little or Nothing, we have missed The Revelation to realize that God is in fact calling us to A New Relationship to Understand that it is time for His Temple to be filled with The Fullness of The Spiritual which brings the Manifestation of The Divine Blessing from God.

We've got to be Born in the Understanding, that if we are Children of God, if it is that we have found ourselves to always filling the Gap that God Should Be Filling with Idols, then there can and will never be any Manifestation for The Almighty Father to Do for us that which is Divinely Fixed for us.

An Idol is any and everything that a person has put before God in their lives; therefore, if we are of the Attitude that every time God Brings forth a Season of Little or Nothing meaning that we are Empty, and the First person we call to bail us out of the situation is a Friend or a Family member or the Pastor of your Church, and it is found that the Last person we choose to acknowledge is God, then it is with this Manifestation that we have placed IDOLS in the Position that God should be Occupying. And by doing this, we have found ourselves in a Cycle that keeps repeating itself until we have fully learnt what it is to Put God First in Everything that we do.

The Lord Reveals that unless a person have found their Relationship with God to be THE FIRST and THE BEST, then that person will never Understand The Mystery of what God Is Doing when God Brings forth a Season of Empty in Our Lives, also Called THE ALONE TIME WITH GOD.

I Hope this Message has been A Blessing for My Readers, I hope that it has brought forth a Divine Revelation to the Minds of God People. I Give All Honor and Praise to The Savior of Mankind, Jesus Christ The Lamb of God. From your Friend Pastor Lerone Dinnall.

THE MYSTERY OF BEING EMPTY.

RECEIVING THE SPIRIT OF OBEDIENCE

Message # 21   **Written in the year 2015.**

ALL PRAISE BE UNTO The Power of Jesus Christ, The True Manifestation of God in the flesh; that came forth to ensure that we have life abundantly. I Greet all My Father's Children in The Wonderful Name of Jesus Christ. Happy am I to be sharing with you another wonderful Message Inspired by The God of Abraham, Isaac and Israel.

1 Timothy Chapter 3:16.

"AND WITHOUT CONTROVERSY GREAT IS THE MYSTERY OF GODLINESS: GOD WAS MANIFEST IN THE FLESH, JUSTIFIED IN THE SPIRIT, SEEN OF ANGELS, PREACHED UNTO THE GENTILES, BELIEVED ON IN THE WORLD, RECEIVED UP INTO GLORY".

As The Topic says, Receiving The Spirit of Obedience: What does this means, and how do I approach A Message like this? The first thing I observed when I got this Message, was to consider the reason for this Message. Think about it, if God Is Going to Give A Message or A Topic unto a people or His People concerning the danger of not being Obedient; does this not raise an alarm in our Mind and Heart to say that, there is danger ahead for someone or a nation that they will be tempted or is already tempted that they should disobey; and not do that which The Lord Has Commanded them to Do.

Well; this is exactly what this Topic is saying unto me; and because I've realize that this is the meaning of the Topic, I now find myself first, in a Searching and an Awareness Mood, that I began searching myself to make sure that I know exactly what is my approach towards any decision that is going to be made by me; to make sure that whatever I am doing, it must be first in The Will of God and not outside of His Will. Because to be in His Will is to be Obedient to His Commands; to be outside of His Will is to be Disobedient to His Commandment.

Let us learn this major lesson in life, the only time we Displease God is when we Disobey God, thus declaring to ourselves that the only Sin there is, is the Sin of Disobedience, if it is that were advancing beyond the Foundational Sin, that being the Sin of Envy that begins in The spiritual part of a man, which is the Mind. Genesis Chapter 2:16-17, Genesis Chapter 3:1-19. The sooner we learn this lesson is the better it will be for us as Children of God. Many Saints of God as not yet come to the understanding that, every time we fail to do what God Command us to Do, it put further Delays on us to receive The Blessing that God Has Promised to Bless us with.

If we should consider it, if God Has in His Plans to Take one (1) year to Fulfill our Blessings, then it must be understood that we are the Blockage that allows that Blessing to be delayed for a longer time, because we did not Obey that which God Commanded us to carry out, in the exact way that God Asked us to Do it. Numbers Chapter 13, speaks of how God Commanded Moses to choose twelve (12) men, a man from each tribe of Israel, to go forth and to spy out the land of Cannon, the land that God Has Already Declared that it is The Inheritance of The Children of Israel.

Now because of that same word Disobedience, The Promised Blessing which should have taken one (1) week at least for them to enter to inherit; was now turned into (40) years, and the length of time was not even the main problem, because those that were living in that generation, all of them died; and their children were the ones that got to see and inherit that which their parents should have inherited. Caleb and Joshua were the only two (2) men that got to see and inherit the Promised Land, because their report was different from that of the other ten (10) men. There are many times we as Children of God are guilty of this saying:

"GOD HAS ALREADY DECLARED MY BLESSING OUT OF HIS MOUTH, THEREFORE NO ONE CAN STOP IT".

In some ways we are right to a Level, but if we don't understand the conditions of our Blessings, then we will be in a Position that we have found ourselves standing in the path of our own Blessings. And the Blessing will stay right there, already Declared, but not yet Decreed upon our life until we have actually received The Spirit of Obedience that will enable us to do exactly what God Need for us to Do.

God Has Blessings for each and every one of His Children, but it always comes with Conditions Applied. Let's look at this story in The Book of Judges Chapter 13. This story is speaking of the promised birth of one of God's Instrument in The Bible; this person is known as Samson. The story goes like this in a summary format; there was a man known as Manoah whose wife was barren, however The Angel of The Lord Appeared unto Manoah's wife, and declared unto her that she was going to conceive and bring forth a son; The Angel also gave her specific Instructions from God that they needed to carry out in order to receive the Blessing. When Manoah heard of this Message, he Prayed to God, that God Would Send back this same Messenger so that he could hear of the Instructions that are to be carried out, so that they would receive this wonderful Blessing. This he did; to put emphasis on how determined he was to ensure that he not only received The Declared Blessing, but to make sure that he received The Decreed Blessing.

The Blessing Remains Declared until we do what God Asked for us to Do; then once we have come up to God's Requirements, then and only then, will The Blessing Be Decreed upon our lives. This man Manoah, gave us an example so that we can know what we should be doing when God Gives us an Instruction for us to Receive His Blessing.

Let's take a look on the contrast of two (2) Scriptures, between two different persons and their attitude towards Obeying God's Word. The first Scripture is Genesis Chapter 22:1-12. This Scripture Clearly Demonstrates that God Did Tempt Abraham, by Asking him to offer his only son, the promised son Isaac, for a burnt offering upon a mountain. What was amazing about Abraham's Attitude was the fact that he demonstrated a Camel like Attitude; he may not have even known the type of attitude a Camel possess. The Bible Said that Abraham, after receiving Instructions from God, rose up early in the morning and saddled his ass, and went on his way to do what God Had Commanded him to Do.

Now, what surprized me about his story, was that Abraham was married, and The Bible Didn't Say that he had a conversation with his wife regarding what God Told him to Do. Because probably if he had told her, she would have tried to restrict him from doing what God Ask him to Do. This passage taught me a lesson that I must always observe; the lesson is: Whenever God Gives us an Instruction to carry out, we must make sure that we are focused on that Message so that no one distract us from carrying out our Mission.

Look at what happen to Peter when he lost his focused, after he was walking on the water; St. Matthew Chapter 14:22-33. Samson lost his strength when he lost focused and put his trust in a woman, rather than what God Instructed his parents to teach him to ensure that he remained undefeated. Judges Chapter 16:1-22. In The Book of 1 Kings Chapter 13. There was a prophet known as the disobedient prophet; God Gave him a charge that he failed to carry out, he was afterwards killed by a lion, whose only purpose was to kill him because he Disobeyed The Voice of God.

If we should continue to read the story of Abraham, we would realize that this man was focused, in carrying out that which God Had Commanded him to Do. Let's look at this a little deeper, when it is that we are going through our Trials and our Testing, it's not the same as Abraham's Test, because we already know about Abraham's story; we already know that every trial is fixed, that we must be overcomers, as long as we Depend on God; we know that The Battle is not ours, it is The Lord's. Abraham on the other hand had no Stories, no Bible, and no Manuscript; but still he was determined despite the odds. Because of faith in God, he passed the Test. His reward is seen in the same Genesis Chapter 22:15-18.

"AND THE ANGEL OF THE LORD CALLED UNTO ABRAHAM OUT OF HEAVEN THE SECOND TIME, AND SAID, BY MYSELF HAVE I SWORN, SAITH THE LORD, FOR BECAUSE THOU HAST DONE THIS THING, AND HAST NOT WITHHELD THY SON, THINE ONLY SON: THAT IN BLESSING I WILL BLESS THEE, AND IN MULTIPLYING I WILL MULTIPLY THY SEED AS THE STARS OF THE HEAVEN, AND AS THE SAND WHICH IS UPON THE SEA SHORE; AND THY SEED SHALL POSSESS THE GATE OF HIS ENEMIES; AND IN THY SEED SHALL ALL THE NATIONS OF THE EARTH BE BLESSED; BECAUSE THOU HAST OBEYED MY VOICE".

It is important for us to remember that after we have Passed The Test and have done that which is Commanded of us to do, then it will be unveiled the Rewards. And the rewards are always greater than the Test. Abraham had A Spirit of Obedience.

The other Scripture that shows the Attitude towards God's Instruction is taken from 1 Samuel Chapter 13:1-14. This story is speaking of king Saul. Now according to the story, it would suggest that Samuel the prophet instructed Saul to tarry for seven (7) days, after which he Samuel would come and make a Sacrifice before God on behalf of Saul to allow his kingdom to continue. The Bible Declares that Saul got impatient, and went ahead and did the Sacrifice himself; now if we read The Bible in Leviticus Chapter 16:29-34, we would have discovered that the actions of Saul was indeed foolish; just as Samuel uttered out of his mouth.

The first thing to recognize is that it was the duty and sole purpose of The Priest to offer the Sacrifice for the atonement of the people; therefore, when Saul went ahead and did it by himself, he was showing complete disrespect towards God's Commandment. Let's look at the mind set of king Saul:

"I AM ALREADY KING, I CAN DO WHATEVER I FEEL LIKE, WHENEVER I FEEL LIKE, AND AT WHAT TIME I FEEL LIKE DOING IT".

If we should speak the truth, many of us were of the Mindset or spirit that king Saul had. Being without Understanding.

With that being said, we now get to realize the Attitude and spirits that affects us at times. I believe that this is the purpose for this Message, so that we can Mortify those type of behaviours and spirits, which is not of God; get it out of our lives. And until we have come to the knowledge of the Truth, that we need to get rid of those type of spirits, we will never be able to receive The Spirit of Obedience. Many of us, this is what is expressed from our Character:

"I AM RESPONSIBLE FOR MYSELF; I PULL MY OWN DOOR AND I HAVE MY OWN MONEY, WHO CAN TALK TO ME; I AM COMPLETE".

We are reminded of The Scripture when the Disciples were discussing about who will be the greatest in The Kingdom of Heaven; what did Jesus do? He called a little child in their midst and Told them:

"EXCEPT YOU BE CONVERTED AND BECOME AS LITTLE CHILDREN, YE CANNOT ENTER THE KINGDOM OF HEAVEN".

We are always reminded that we need to be as humble as a child, because this is God's Requirement. This is The Spirit that God Need us to have.

Let us not be like king Nebuchadnezzar in The Book of Daniel Chapter 4. God Had to Humble king Nebuchadnezzar for him to realize, that only God Is God. And also king Manasseh had a similar experience in The Book of 2 Chronicles Chapter 33:1-20. God is Seeking for individuals who are willing to Change for His Will, and to be Born in His Spirit, therefore, allowing us to Receive that Spirit of Obedience.

King Saul found out the hard way, that the title of king did not immune him from being Obedient to God's Commandment. His punishment was rejection from being king, and not only him, but his entire generation was Rejected. Let me ask this Question: Are we willing to Disobey God that He Will Curse not only us, but also our generation to follow? _____.

I don't think I will take that chance, therefore I'm Praying to God that He Will Teach me how to be Humble, and that I may adapt in order to Receive The Spirit of Obedience.

It is truly sad to say this, but I have A Message to deliver, therefore I have to say what The Lord is Saying. This is it: There is a lot of people who will not receive this Spirit of Obedience, and I'm talking about people that are considered to be Saved and are currently going to Church. Truth be told there is a lot of people that have Rejected the call to be Obedient to The Spirit and Voice of God, therefore it is found that God Has Rejected many people because of Disobedience.

I would like for us to read The Book of Jeremiah Chapter 5:20-25. And also Isaiah Chapter 6:9-13. These Scriptures Clearly Demonstrate that God Has Declared over the lives of many who are Disobedient, a spirit that they will continue to be Disobedient; a spirit that they will not hear the Gospel to be Saved; a spirit that they will not even see the signs of the time, to know that His coming is near; a spirit that their ears will be heavy to hear; a spirit that will cause them to have no respect for God or God's People. Romans Chapter 1:21-32, Speaks of how God Turn people like these who don't Obey Him, over to a Reprobate Mind, to do those things which are not convenient.

There is something special that I need for us to remember; this is it: It is said that when a person has fully learnt, it is demonstrated in their Attitude, because their Attitude would have also learnt A New Behaviour. Therefore, if we have received The Spirit of Obedience, it means that we have learnt how to be Obedient, and our Attitude must resemble Obedience. If we Declare that we are Obeying God and our Attitude which brings forth our Character is different from that which The Word of God Says; then the truth is that we have not yet Received The Spirit of Obedience, thus our Character remains the same.

I recently had an experience and I would like to share it with The

People of God, regarding Obedience; I happen to be doing a lot of work lately, therefore I find myself going to bed at about 2-4 A.M. In the mornings; you would think that, going to your bed at that time, no one would even have a chance to disturb you out of your sleep; until you have received your full dose of sleep. Then you find out that it is your only daughter that is not feeling well, that makes you find the energy to get up, to ensure that she is well. I had to make a necessary sacrifice, to ensure that my daughter is taken care of. So is it with Obedience, we need to have an Attitude, that we look on Obedience as A NECESSARY SACRIFICE, even when it is so difficult to do.

You may ask yourself this Question: What is it that God Needs me to do? _____

_____.

That Answer is a personal answer between you and God. But this is what I would say, read The Book of Deuteronomy Chapter 6. And Deuteronomy Chapter 8. And also The Book of Micah Chapter 6:1-8. These Scripture will give us a general idea of what God's Requirements are.

Am I doing all that I need to be doing, to remain in Obedience with God? _____. And I will Repeat, this is a Question only you can Answer.

May God Continue to Bless you, Keep you and Prosper you. I hope this Message have blessed your life. All Power Belongs to Jesus Christ, The True Manifestation of God.

From The Servant of God, Pastor Lerone Dinnall.

RECEIVING THE SPIRIT OF OBEDIENCE.

THE LORD WILL PROVIDE

JEHOVAH-JIREH; YAHWEH WILL PROVIDE.

Message # 51　　　　　　**Date Started January 30, 2017.**
　　　　　　　　　　　　　Date Finalized February 3, 2017.

GENESIS CHAPTER 22:7-14.

"AND ISAAC SPAKE UNTO ABRAHAM HIS FATHER, AND SAID, MY FATHER: AND HE SAID, HERE AM I, MY SON. AND HE SAID, BEHOLD THE FIRE AND THE WOOD: BUT WHERE IS THE LAMB FOR A BURNT OFFERING? AND ABRAHAM SAID, MY SON, GOD WILL PROVIDE HIMSELF A LAMB FOR A BURNT OFFERING: SO THEY WENT BOTH OF THEM TOGETHER. AND THEY CAME TO THE PLACE WHICH GOD HAD TOLD HIM OF; AND ABRAHAM BUILT AN ALTAR THERE, AND LAID THE WOOD IN ORDER, AND BOUND ISAAC HIS SON, AND LAID HIM ON THE ALTAR UPON THE WOOD. AND ABRAHAM STRETCHED FORTH HIS HAND, AND TOOK THE KNIFE TO SLAY HIS SON. AND THE ANGEL OF THE LORD

CALLED UNTO HIM OUT OF HEAVEN, AND SAID, ABRAHAM,
ABRAHAM: AND HE SAID, HERE AM I. AND HE SAID, LAY NOT
THINE HAND UPON THE LAD, NEITHER DO THOU ANYTHING
UNTO HIM: FOR NOW I KNOW THAT THOU FEAREST GOD,
SEEING THOU HAST NOT WITHHELD THY SON, THINE ONLY SON
FROM ME. AND ABRAHAM LIFTED UP HIS EYES, AND LOOKED,
AND BEHOLD BEHIND HIM A RAM CAUGHT IN A THICKET BY
HIS HORNS: AND ABRAHAM WENT AND TOOK THE RAM, AND
OFFERED HIM UP FOR A BURNT OFFERING IN THE STEAD OF
HIS SON. AND ABRAHAM CALLED THE NAME OF THAT PLACE
JEHOVAH-JIREH: AS IT IS SAID TO THIS DAY, IN THE MOUNT OF
THE LORD IT SHALL BE SEEN".

I CALL UPON THE GOD OF ABRAHAM, ISAAC AND ISRAEL;
THE GOD THAT ASKED ABRAHAM A SIMPLE QUESTION, BECAUSE
IT WAS SIMPLE TO HIM; AND GOD ASKED ABRAHAM:

"IS ANYTHING TOO HARD FOR THE LORD?"

LORD I PRAY AT THIS MOMENT IN THIS MESSAGE FOR ALL
TIMES, THAT GOD WHO IS KNOWN AS THE ONLY LIVING GOD;
WILL AT THIS TIME AND EVEN FOREVERMORE RELEASE AN
ANOINTING OF POWER AND AUTHORITY TO THE MINDS OF
ALL THOSE WHO WILL COME IN CONTACT WITH THE READING
OF THIS MESSAGE, THAT THIS MESSAGE WILL EMPOWER THE
READERS TO BELIEVE AND TO ACT BY FAITH, TO KNOW, THAT
NO MATTER WHAT THE ENEMY THROWS THEIR DIRECTION, ON
THE PATHWAY THAT YOUR PEOPLE TRAVELS ON, THAT YOUR
PEOPLE WHICH ARE CALLED BY YOUR NAME WILL BELIEVE TO
EXPRESS THE CONFIDENT SHOWN BY THE FATHER OF FAITH
ABRAHAM; TO KNOW THAT SOMEHOW, SOMEWHERE, AT ANY
HOUR, AT ANY MINUTE, AT ANY SECOND, THAT THE GOD OF THE
UNIVERSE WILL, WILL, MUST, MUST, MUST COME THROUGH
AND DELIVER FOR THE RIGHTEOUS SEED. LORD I RECALL YOU
SPOKE BY THE MOUTH OF DAVID TO UTTER THE WORDS THAT
SAYS:

"I HAVE BEEN YOUNG, AND NOW AM OLD; YET HAVE I NOT

SEEN THE RIGHTEOUS FORSAKEN, NOR HIS SEED BEGGING BREAD".

LORD I PRAY EVEN RIGHT NOW IN THE NAME OF JESUS CHRIST, THAT NO MATTER HOW DARK AND LONELY THE ROAD GETS, YOU WILL MOVE BY YOUR SPIRIT IN THE LIVES OF THOSE WHO BELIEVE IN GOD, TO MANIFEST THE MOVEMENT OF YOUR ANOINTING TO SEPARATE EVERY RED SEA; LORD THAT YOU WILL BRING EVERY VALLEY HIGH FOR YOUR PEOPLE; LORD THAT YOU WILL PULL DOWN EVERY MOUNTAINS IN THE LIVES OF YOUR PEOPLE; LORD I PRAY THAT YOU WILL BRAKE EVERY PRINCIPALITIES AND POWERS FROM OFF THE MIND OF YOUR PEOPLE, TO LET US HOPE AGAIN, TO LET US HAVE FAITH AGAIN IN GOD, TO COME INTO THE BELIEF, THAT GOD WILL OPEN THOSE DOORS WHICH WERE CONSIDERED CLOSE, AND TO REBUKE THE POWERS OF FALLEN ANGELS THAT SEEKS TO STOP THE BLESSINGS THAT FLOWS THROUGH THE WINDOWS OF HEAVEN.

LORD, ALLOW US TO BELIEVE IN THE GOD THAT WORKED FOR ELIJAH AMONGST FOUR HUNDRED PROPHET OF BAAL, THAT YOU'RE STILL GOD THAT LIVETH AND WALKETH WITH US IN THE DARKEST NIGHT WE COULD EVER ENCOUNTER. LORD JESUS CHRIST I PRAY THAT THIS MESSAGE WILL CHANGE LIVES, WILL GIVE CONFIDENCE AND HOPE TO ALL THOSE WHO TRUST IN THE GOD OF ABRAHAM, ISAAC AND ISRAEL; THAT WE MAY TRUST IN THE BLOOD THAT YOU SHED ON THE CROSS, TO WALK IN THE BELIEF EACH DAY, AND HAVE THE CONFIDENCE TO DECLARE AND TO DECREE OVER OUR LIVES THAT THE LORD WHO IS OUR JEHOVAH-JIREH, JESUS CHRIST WILL PROVIDE FOR HIS PEOPLE. I PRAY ONLY IN THE NAME OF JESUS CHRIST.

BE BLESSED, WHILE GOD CONTINUES TO BLESS HIS PEOPLE. THE LORD WILL PROVIDE, THE LORD WILL PROVIDE, THE LORD WILL PROVIDE, AMEN.

I Greet My Lord and Saviour Jesus Christ, The All Powerful and Mighty God; Privileged am I to write this Message, of which I know that it will be of Great benefit to those who read. This Message came forth by means of A Test that I had to go through, in order to realize that as the Message describes and acknowledge, The Lord Will Provide. I know we all know that The God that we are Serving is A Provider, but, is that belief been Born in our lives; have we seen it for ourselves, to bring forth the Experience to know that God Is Indeed God for our lives. Have we passed the Level of knowing God through the Reading of His Word, and now Elevated to beginning to know God by our everyday actions of life; because God Must Manifest His Likeness all over the life we now live for Him, for us to know Him as God.

I've experienced something recently, I did a job, of which no one else would desire to do, because that's the person God Made me to be, I love a challenge; and upon doing this job, there were certain items that were needed for this job, that the customer at that time could not find the necessary funding to purchase all that is required; of which they asked me if I could stand the expense, and repair the Vehicle, and by giving me their sworn promise that they will honor the payments of the repairs for the Motor Vehicle; this I agreed to do.

I finished the repairs for the Vehicle and was promised the first installment of payment for that month end, of which I got less than what was bargain for that person to pay; the following month the client called me to let me know that he will not be able to pay me what is balanced on the bill, because he did some checks and realized that my cost for repairing his Vehicle was more than what other Technicians would have cost, and also found out that the Materials was also more expensive than what the Suppliers was selling them for; therefore for that reason he will not be paying me more than what others would have charged.

NOTE: I made over five trips into Kingston for this Client Vehicle, back and forth; Trip to Machine shop; trips to four different Part suppliers, just to ensure that I got all the Materials I needed to do a perfect Job.

I listen on the phone for a good five minutes before I made any response, because I just could not believe what I was hearing. The first conversation I had with this Client is to let him know after the assessment of his Vehicle was done, to let him understand that the Repairs was going to cost money; of which he begged me to please do the Repairs, and he would faithfully honor the Responsibilities of the Bill. The Bill was even signed by this Client with a promise that he would fulfill his Responsibilities.

Being on the Phone listening to this Client, realizing to myself that the money he owed me was already spent, to do what was required for it to do, even though I haven't received it in my hands. I looked to The Heavens, with a thought in My Mind Asking God, if He Sees and Hear what is happening. Then it was like The Birth of A New Confidence, A New Faith to Declare and to Decree over that very Situation, in that very Atmosphere; and I open my mouth for the first time being on the phone; because I was in such a shock, by hearing what was coming out of the mouth of this Client; I told the Client to do what seems best to him; I told him to continue to do all his checks, and to make sure that he also check to see that the Vehicle was worked on, and is in perfect condition from what it was. I told him that if by his calculations he found out that I should not get one penny more, then just do what seems best in his judgment.

I said to this Client, The God that I Serve Will Always Fill the gap; if I'm to get $10,000 in a day, and someone that should give that $10,000 chooses to only to give $5,000. Then don't worry, My God Will Send someone else with the other $5,000 to ensure that my daily provisions is met, don't worry, do what seems fit in your eyes, as for me, The Lord Will Provide.

These words came as a surprise to me, because I knew they weren't my words, but The Words of The God that Liveth In me. Saints, the greatest pain of this experience is to know that I took time out to go on the road, to assist this Client, when the Vehicle was unable to move; but The Lord Revealed to me by Saying:

"I KNOW IT HURTS, BUT I WILL PROVIDE; THE LORD WILL PROVIDE".

When I had a good look on what took place, even though it hurts, because I took most of my personal money to buy materials to correct the problem with the engine of this Client's Vehicle; and not to mention the amount of time and the use of my personal transportation to go around from Machine shop to Parts suppliers. I felt like Asaph, when he said, my feet almost slipped. When I had an overall look on the situation, I Gave God Thanks, because, if it weren't for that Test, I would not have witness The Birth of A New and Fresh Anointing, that Spoke to me in the midst of that Storm, to Let me know that God Sees, and He have Sent His Word, which Says:

"PEACE BE STILL, THE LORD WILL PROVIDE".

The Customer kept on saying to me, I know you feel bad, but this is what he decided to do, and also asking if I had any arguments; and I kept on saying; do what is considered best in your eyes.

Thank you Jesus Christ, I have Proven You to Be My Lord and Saviour, My JEHOVAH-JIREH one more time.

I recall explaining a particular Topic to someone in The Church that should be very helpful for this Message. I remember speaking to a Prophetess, and I was explaining to this Sister, that when The Lord Desires to Speak to His People, and if there is found in The Assembly of God those that are Prophets and Prophetess; The Lord Then Choose A Vessel from those who will speak, depending on the nature of The Message that is to be Delivered, and also with the condition that those who will speak, meets The Requirement of Holiness to be Used by God. I remember explaining to this person that if God Chooses a person to use for example, for the benefit of Admonishing The Church; if it is that, that Individual chooses to quench The Spirit of God; what it means it that God Will then Move His Anointing to Speak, from that Person, to another Available Vessel that is more than willing to Declare and Decree Thus Saith The Lord.

And so it is, when God Send forth His Anointing of Favors for A Child of God to be Blessed by Provisions to meet their daily demand, if it is that a person who God Has Chosen to bring forth a Financial Aid for A Child of God by means of that Child of God doing some Repairs to that person's Vehicle or any other work; if that person then chooses to quench the Operation of The Movement of God for their life to be Blessed with Financial Benefits, that The Sons of God should be Blessed; then don't worry, because God Is THE **BEST**

CHESS PLAYER; God Will then Move that person away, and put someone else in place, that will be more than willing to carry out that which God Command for His People.

There is an Example that I can give to make God's People understand how Important we are to God and to life's every production. This Example is going to be a Comparison of a Motor Vehicle to that of our Christian Life.

In the Automotive Field we are train on the studies of how a Vehicles Engine Operates; now in an Engine there is one word that is mainly used to describe an Engine, and that word is known as Efficiency, which in a nut shell means how effective the use of the Engine is and can be, and to enable that Engine to maintain an 100% Efficiency at all times. The Engine is designed to create Power to enable the Vehicle to move; in each cylinder of the Engine, there is a Standard 16:1 ratio of Air and Gas to create the power that is necessary to accumulate the word Efficiency. 16 part of Air to 1 part of Gas.

Now there are times when problems will occurs in the Engine that will not support the cylinder receiving 16:1 ratio; and it is found that only 10 parts of Air is available; now the Engine cannot produce power if the full portions is not supplied, therefore, the Vehicle is also equipped with a Master Computer, which checks every information that is taking place with the Vehicle, and if it is that the Computer senses that there is a low production of Air, which should be 16 part, because the cylinder must be filled with a ratio of 16:1; the Computer then makes some small adjustments, by placing 7 part of Gas, which should originally be 1 part, to accommodate for the loss of the 6 part of Air that was not provided to ensure that the cylinder is filled, to ensure that power is obtained, to ensure that work is done by the Vehicle at the highest standard. It must be noted however that the Computer first realize that the Engine is under performing, before it takes steps to make adjustments.

I'm not certain how many of My Readers would have understood the theory I just explained; but to allow us to understand better, let me reveal the comparison:

The Engine / Vehicle would represent The Children of God; that which supplies the Engine / Children of God to perform, would represent The Favors or The Blessings from God Above; those things that prevent the Engine / Children of God from performing the way it should perform, would be the Adversaries, the Fight that we face to survive, Principalities, Powers, Spiritual Wickedness in high places, Fallen Angels, The Demons that possess our Employers, and those that give us work to perform and turn around don't want to pay us, to see if we are going to melt, and begin to underperform for God in Worship.

The work that the Engine / Children of God should perform, is our Worship before God, for us to live the life that God Has Destined for us to live. The Master Computer for the Engine / Children of God would represent The Almighty God, which Sees everything and Knows everything; and also Monitor every movement of A Child of God, and whenever it is that we are underperforming because of the Elements that exist, Our Father then makes the necessary Adjustments, to enable us to perform again the way we were built to Perform, because God Knows us better than anyone else.

The supplies the Master Computer takes to make the necessary adjustment for the Engine / Children of God to again perform; to Satisfy the Engine needs, this is every and any Provisions the World has stored up, not realizing that they are only storing those provisions for The Children of God; because The Righteous shall inherit the Land; the Earth is The Lords and the Fullness thereof, the World and all therein is.

Whenever it is that we know for a fact that we are not Worshipping God the way God is to be Worshipped; God Also Knows, and He's Making the necessary Adjustments for us to get back to the place that we can Worship the way God Built us to Worship Him, which is Spirit and Truth, and that type of Worship marks 100% Efficiency in God Eyes.

NOTE: It is also important to understand that just as it is that the Master Computer first has to confirm for a while that the necessary provisions is not being supplied to the engine; so is it with God, He

Has to Confirm for a surety, that those whom He Had Set in place to supply for our needs are not doing what He Had Commanded for them to Do, thus He Can Make the necessary adjustments for another person to supply our daily provisions. Therefore, in Serving God, Patience is very important, because God May Delay, but that doesn't mean that God Will not be right on time to Deliver His People.

According to The Book of 1st Samuel, Saul was chosen to be king and he did Became king, and would have remain being A king, if he had the Disciple to do all that God Required for him to Do; we know the story, he disobeyed a Direct Command from God, spoken by the mouth of Samuel The Prophet. Did this action by Saul Shocked God, did it Stopped God's Rule and Desires from being Accomplished? No it didn't. God Then Told Samuel to Go and offer a Sacrifice, and invite the House of Jesse, because He Had Chosen Himself A king, A king unlike Saul; this king will carry out All His Desires and Command; that king was known as David, a little Shepherd boy, that they never even called to come to the Sacrifice, because according to man's eye, David the Youngest could not be the one that God Had Chosen. And speaking about David, there is an important Revelation to realize from the life of David, that can be shown to us, to make us understand the Importance of The Children of God Being and remaining to Be The Righteous Seed. According to The Book of 1st Samuel Chapter 16. After David was Chosen by God to be the new king of Israel, of which he had to wait on God's Time.

It is Reported in this very Chapter, Verse 14. That The Spirit of The Lord Departed from Saul, and an evil spirit from The Lord Troubled him. It was then advised to Saul that he needed someone in whom The Spirit of God Was Upon, to play the musical Instrument called an Harp; and by doing this, the evil spirit which troubled king Saul would depart from him for a Season. King Saul gave permission to his Advisors to seek for such a man in whom The Spirit of God Is Upon. In Verse 18, it was told king Saul by one of his servants, that they have seen a son of Jesse the Bethlehemite, that is cunning in playing, and a mighty valiant man, and a man of war and prudent in matters, and a comely person, and most important the servant said that The Lord Is With him.

The remainder of The Scripture Tells of how Saul invited David to play the Harp, of which when he played, the evil spirit that came from God Departed from Saul, which made Saul realized that he had to keep David around; he made David his Armourbearer; therefore, whenever the evil spirit came upon king Saul, he asked David to play the Harp which brought forth a release for a Season of the Torments he suffered at The Hands of God.

We wonder at times how it is that The Righteous Seed receive some jobs that we are just not Qualified to perform, but still without any fight, we walk into Positions that someone who was trained for years had occupied.

The Bible Never Mentioned that David got training to be an Armourbearer; The Bible Said that he kept the sheeps; and because it is now Proven that The Spirit of God Is Upon Him, the Only Spirit that Grants Favors and Brings Forth A Cleansing; king Saul had to keep David around, not knowing that he was Fulfilling God's Purpose of Training the New king.

So it is with us that are Righteous Seed; we will remain in Jobs, and keep on receiving Promotions, until we become the Head, because that's the only way to keep us in the Job, to Allow God's Favors to continually Be Upon that Organization.

I Pray that we will now understand that Being The Righteous Seed, we don't need to run down and seek to compete with the World for the Best Qualification there is to get, in order for God to Give us the Best Jobs; it is very simple, all God Asked from us is to be Obedient to His Words, as it is Mentioned in The Book of St Matthew Chapter 6:33. The Lord Said:

"BUT SEEK YE FIRST THE KINGDOM OF GOD, AND HIS RIGHTEOUSNESS; AND ALL THESE THINGS SHALL BE ADDED UNTO YOU".

When God Identify that we have been Obedient and have seek for His Righteousness; then and only then will we be able to step into Positions that others are just occupying for now. Psalms 127:1 Says:

"EXCEPT THE LORD BUILD THE HOUSE, THEY LABOUR IN VAIN THAT BUILD IT: EXCEPT THE LORD KEEP THE CITY, THE WATCHMAN WAKETH BUT IN VAIN".

The problem that many of us as Christians fail to realize is that, it is not one or two Seasons of doing what God Asked us to Do is Accepted in God's Eyes; but God Requires from His People A Continual Effort to Become Righteous; we are not going to get everything right at the first, second or third attempt, and even longer; but it is important for us to understand that God Is Seeking for those who will Become Righteous Seed only to have the Earnest Desires of Needing to Do the Right things; and even when we attempt to do the Right things, and it is not seen in man's eye of being of that Character; but in God's Eyes He Sees the True Intentions.

It is mentioned in The Bible that the servants of Saul said that they saw Upon the Life of David, that God Was With him.

QUESTION: Even though it is known that we are Baptized and going to Church; Giving our Tithes and Offerings; Visiting the Sick, the Fatherless and Widows, and anything else we have as an Activity for The Ministry of God's Kingdom; here is the True Question:

"IS GOD WITH US, THAT IT CAN BE SEEN BY OTHERS, TO KNOW THAT WE ARE OF THE RIGHTEOUS SEED"? _____.

There is a lesson here to learn for those of us who are Children of God, and is in constant Expectation for God to Provide.

1. Remain being A Child that Serve The Almighty God.
2. Be Patient with God; even though David was Anointed to be king, he still had to wait on The Fulfillment of God's Time.
3. When God Send forth His Blessings upon our Lives, even if it is our Employer that is given the Command to Bless our Lives, if that Employer desires for God to Continue to Bless his life and his Business, then that Employer will humbly submit to God's every Command for God's Child to be Blessed by the means of that Employer's Business.

4. God Sends Forth Favors on the Land, in Business, only because of The Righteous Seed; Yes, that's True! If there were no Righteous Seed, there will be no Favors from God. Just look at what happen to king Ahab and his wife Jezebel and the Kingdom that they ruled in their time; God Refused to Send Rain on the land because those who ruled were not Righteous but Ungodly. 1 Kings Chapter 18. Therefore, I take this opportunity to speak to The Righteous Seed; BE CONFIDENT, continue to lift your eyes to The Hills, from whence cometh your Help, because God Will Not Fail us; God Do Not Know how to Fail; Failure is not a word in God's Dictionary; Failure is compared to Sin in God's Eye, He Will Never Come close to it. Righteousness Exalted A Nation, but sin is a reproach to any people; therefore let us embrace Righteousness. It is time for God's People to Know their Position in Life, especially if we know without doubt, that we are in fact The Righteous Seed. And being The Righteous Seed is not a word we repeat, but it is a lifestyle.

5. We are so Important to God, that even if one door closes, God Will Provide many other doors, that we never even knew existed, by means of someone else that we were not counting on.

6. Remember that The Lord Will Provide; The Lord Will Provide; The Lord Must Provide for The Righteous Seed.

7. Just wait on God's Provision, because Frustration may occur if we are not Disciplined to be Patient for God's Time, and if we become frustrated, this will lead us to walk out of The Will of God, to establish our own destiny, of which there is no Purposeful Destiny outside of God's Will.

It is Ironic to know that the World has identified and know for a Fact, that when they have in their place of Business a person who is A Righteous Seed; Employers now know that their Business will expand because of The Favors that Flows from God because The Righteous Seed is a part of their Organization. And guess what? There are many of us, who have not yet been Born to the realization that because we are of The Righteous Seed, our very Presence allow The Light of God to Shine into whatever we put our hands to. Therefore, because we do not know the value of Who we are, and Who's we are; we become adjusted to the belief the World has spoon feed us with, to make us believe that we are just like any other Employee, which is A Lie.

The Righteous Seed, The True Worshipper, A Child of God can never be like any other Employee; because we are Light, and everyone else around us only seek to aspire to be of the Likeness of Who We Represent. And for this we have to be very careful, because the enemy will always seek to influence the lives of The True Worshippers / Righteous Seed to believe that we are commoners like everyone else, which again I repeat is A LIE.

The Serpent did his best and convinced Eve that there was still the Best that God Refused to Give to her and her Husband, of which she believed in his words which was all a lie and a trap to ensure that both Adam and Eve Lost their Position, The Likeness and Authority in God, Eternity. So it is with us, we must understand that everything that God Has Given to us, is already THE BEST. Therefore, the next time someone comes to us, seeking to influence a change in our Character to make us believe that anyone and everyone can do our job, therefore, we should change from our standards and take less pay than that which we desire as a satisfactory payment for our Righteous Seed Labour; Rebuke them; Yes, I said it, Rebuke them, and even if we have not reach The Anointing of the Level in God to openly rebuke with our mouths; we must make sure that we flush that Garbage information from our Minds, Heart and spirit; and look towards feeding our spirit with The Word of God that Declares to us that we are Righteous Priesthood, Holy Nation and A Peculiar People. Because even though someone seeks to do what The Righteous Seeds are doing, in the same pattern that we have done it; it can never bring forth the same results; because The Calling and Anointing of God is upon our Lives Which Says:

Genesis Chapter 12:2&3.

"AND I WILL MAKE OF THEE A GREAT NATION, AND I WILL

BLESS THEE, AND MAKE THY NAME GREAT; AND THOU SHALT
BE A BLESSING: AND I WILL BLESS THEM THAT BLESS THEE,
AND CURSE HIM THAT CURSETH THEE: AND IN THEE SHALL
ALL FAMILIES OF THE EARTH BE BLESSED".

Now it is important for us to understand that although these
words were spoken to Abraham directly; it is written for us to
understand that THE **QUALIFIED STATE** of that which Abraham
found himself to be in, because of Obedience, to Release God's Favor
and Anointing, not only upon his personal life, but also upon the lives
of all those in the future that will aspire to reach the Qualified State
of which Abraham acquired. Yes, fellow Saints, that Blessing which
was Released upon Abraham is also our Birth Rights, it belongs to us;
and don't allow anyone to tell us anything else than that which was
Pronounced, Declared and Decreed upon Father Abraham.

Let us not be like Esau, which did not know the importance of
The Birth Right, which traded it for a meal; let us be of the Attitude
of Jacob that wrestle with the Angel, and would not let go, until he
received his Blessing.

NOTE: If we are Children of God, our Attitudes must Manifest
that we are Inheritance of God's Blessings. But there is currently
taking place in the World that, the Children of Darkness are seeking
to Imprint in the Minds of The Children of God, that The Blessings
of God which should be The Inheritance of God's Children, are
theirs to have. It doesn't matter how long it takes for God to Begin
to Manifest, our job is to Trust God and have Patience, because The
Lord Will Provide.

I have A Testimony, which I have told to many people before,
and I'm now going to tell My Readers; I am convinced, that God
Has Angels Walking and Living amongst us; reason for me saying
this: there are many times I find myself in situations and conditions,
that cannot be penciled out by man's knowledge; and in those many
times, when I sought The Lord, He Allows someone that I've never
met before, to show up just on time with a Vehicle, and desires for
me to work on their Vehicle, and after the Vehicle is completed, and

I received payments, I don't see that person again, nor can I find that person.

And again there are True Christians in the World that God Has Placed in our lives to be A True Support to help us along lives road. And also there are those who are The True Worshippers that do things in Secret, and you will never know that it was that person that did a good deed because when they did it, they weren't seeing the face of man, but The Face of God.

I know the World is becoming Rough and harder to tolerate; but we must have Faith and Patience; there is still True Worshippers around, and there is still True Worshipper that God Has in Preparation; they may not be at that level as yet, but in time that Level of Anointing and Calling will be Realized. And once there is still the Evidence of The Righteous Seed, God Will Continue to Send Favors for His People to Survive, even if those Favors come in the likeness of a person who we have never seen before. I'm Reading and Studying The Bible, and I'm yet to see where in The Bible it is mention that God Has Failed The Righteous Seed.

God Didn't Failed Adam and Eve, but Adam and Eve Failed God. God Didn't Failed Abraham even when he deceived Pharaoh and Abimelech out of Fear for his Wife, God Still Stood by his side. God Never Failed Isaac or Jacob; and even when Joseph taught that God Had Abandoned him, his latter days proved that God Was Only Setting him up for Greatness. Moses a leader that was concern that he couldn't speak to Represent God; God Did Prove to him that although he had short comings, God Was Stronger than his weakness. No man could stand before Joshua, as it was Declared and Decreed by God. David had an army of Angels every time he went to Battle, thus proving that he was Serving The Only Living God of Israel. Daniel, though Tested with Lions, found out that it was God that Made the Lions to bite. The three Hebrew Boys was justified by their Belief of God, and Proved that not even Fire heated seven times more than what it was meant to be heated could not even harm a hair upon their heads.

Reading and Studying The Bible brings me to The Sure Conclusion to know that The Living God Never Failed in The Past, God Never Fails in The Present and it is a certain that God Will Never Fail in The Future; and through every conditions of life, there is one thing that remains Constant, this is it:

"THE LORD WILL PROVIDE FOR THE RIGHTEOUS SEED".

All Glory and Honor be unto The King of kings and The Lord of lords, Jesus Christ The Lamb of God. I remain your Faithful Minister in The Lord; continue to Pray for me and My Family, as I continue to Pray for your Growth in The Lord. Pastor Lerone Dinnall.

JEHOVAH-JIREH: YAHWEH WILL PROVIDE
THE LORD WILL PROVIDE.

Mountains; Valleys; Storms and Seas; Fire and Water; The Different Challenges of A Christian's Journey

Message # 88　　　　　　**Date Started January 20, 2018**
　　　　　　　　　　　　　Date Finalized January 31, 2018.

St Matthew Chapter 20:20-23.

"Then came to him the mother of Zebedee's children with her sons, worshipping Him, and desiring a certain thing of Him. And He Said unto her, What wilt thou? She saith unto Him, Grant that these my two sons may sit, the one on Thy Right Hand, and the other on The Left, in Thy Kingdom. But Jesus Answered and Said, ye know not what ye ask. Are ye able to drink of the

CUP THAT I SHALL DRINK OF, AND TO BE BAPTIZED WITH THE BAPTISM THAT I AM BAPTIZED WITH? THEY SAY UNTO HIM, WE ARE ABLE. AND HE SAID UNTO THEM, YE SHALL DRINK INDEED OF MY CUP, AND BE BAPTIZED WITH THE BAPTISM THAT I AM BAPTIZED WITH: BUT TO SIT ON MY RIGHT HAND, AND ON MY LEFT, IS NOT MINE TO GIVE, BUT IT SHALL BE GIVEN TO THEM FOR WHOM IT IS PREPARED OF MY FATHER".

I Give Honor to The Only Living God, Jesus Christ The Lamb of God. Happy to be in this Position yet another time to be able to write Inspiring Messages for God's Chosen People. The Bible Made Mentioned of A Scripture that Says:

"MANY ARE CALLED BUT ONLY FEW ARE CHOSEN".

There is a saying that is echoed by many that started this Christian Pathway and was just not able to carry on the journey; the statement goes like this:

"NO ONE TOLD ME THAT IT WAS GOING TO BE SO HARD; NO ONE TOLD ME THAT I WOULD HAVE TO SURRENDER ALL THE BAD HABITS AND ESPECIALLY THOSE THINGS THAT I LOVE TO DO; NO ONE EXPLAINED TO ME THAT IN ORDER TO KEEP SAVED, I WOULD HAVE TO SEEK THE FACE OF GOD ALMIGHTY; THEY NEVER TOLD ME THAT I WOULD HAVE TO CONTINUE TO FEED MY SOUL BY READING THE WORD OF GOD EVERY DAY; THEY NEVER TOLD ME THAT I WOULD HAVE TO BE IN FASTING SERVICES AND PRAYER MEETING AND BIBLE STUDIES; NO ONE TOLD ME THAT THE WALK WITH CHRIST MUST BECOME A WALK FREE FROM FORNICATION AND ADULTERY; NO ONE TOLD ME THAT IN ORDER TO SERVE THE LIVING GOD, I WOULD HAVE TO MAKE SURE THAT I AM SANCTIFY BEFORE MY SACRIFICE CAN BE ACCEPTED; NO ONE TOLD ME, NO ONE TOLD ME!

LET THIS MESSAGE BEAR RECORD THAT SOMEONE HAS TOLD YOU. AND IT MUST BE THE EXPECTATION THAT THERE IS A LOT MORE TO BE SACRIFICED, THAN THAT WHICH IS LISTED HERE FOR THAT PERSON THAT CHOOSE TO WALK THE ROAD OF THE CHRISTIAN'S JOURNEY".

THE LORD SAID: "COME UNTO ME, ALL YE THAT LABOUR

AND ARE HEAVY LADEN, AND I WILL GIVE YOU REST. TAKE MY YOKE UPON YOU, AND LEARN OF ME; FOR I AM MEEK AND LOWLY IN HEART: AND YE SHALL FIND REST UNTO YOUR SOULS. FOR MY YOKE IS EASY, AND MY BURDEN IS LIGHT". St Matthew Chapter 11:28-30.

I am happy for this Message, reason being, I've found out that I spend less time explaining to those who are not Saved, and those who are not yet fully persuaded, because there is A Message that speaks to every condition that a person may or may not be experiencing, that will no doubt lead to that person giving a full surrender of their life over to God when it is that such a person have reached the point of full Surrender.

There is one thing that must always be remembered by those of us who are Preachers and Teachers of The Gospel of Jesus Christ, and that is; Our main Job is to make sure we SOW GOOD SEEDS. There are many that will seek to sow the seed of The Word of God, then water, then fertilize and watch and watch to see if the seed is growing. The Effectiveness of Christianity cannot be established in a man; but rather The Special Ingredience comes only from God The Father. Truth be told, we are Given A Calling to Preach and to Teach to those who will have the appetite to Listen, and there is no way we can understand The Mystery of God to know who will receive of that Seed except God Reveals it to us. We have heard a joyful sound Jesus Saves, Jesus Saves, spread the news all around Jesus Saves, Jesus Saves.

Someone of Authority spoke to me about three months ago, and they wanted to know what is My Teaching Techniques in regards to convincing people to give their lives over to God. I told that person, that I only tell those who are in need of Saving Grace what The Bible Says. The person asked me what if that doesn't work, what will I do next? I replied by saying:

"IF THEY DON'T WANT TO RECEIVE THE WORD OF GOD, THEN I CAN'T HELP THEM".

I also said to that person, that the sad fact to life, is that there will be a lot of people that are already marked to go to hell, and it's always a few in number that are given The Seal of The Father to Inherit Heaven, and that's the Truth. The Season is already upon us which says:

"LET THE RIGHTEOUS BE RIGHTEOUS STILL AND LET THE FILTHY BE FILTHY STILL".

The Bible Says in The Book of Isaiah Chapter 55:6&7.

"SEEK YE THE LORD WHILE HE MAY BE FOUND, CALL YE UPON HIM WHILE HE IS NEAR: LET THE WICKED FORSAKE HIS WAY, AND THE UNRIGHTEOUS MAN HIS THOUGHTS: AND LET HIM RETURN UNTO THE LORD, AND HE WILL ABUNDANTLY PARDON".

Just have a look at the portion of The Scripture that Says: Seek ye The Lord while He may be FOUND! This statement is making reference for me to understand that there will become a time in life that those who were never seeking to find God, there is a time that will be Revealed that even though they will try hard to find God, they will not find God, because there is A Season and A Time for everything under the Sun, and when the Seasons and Time for Salvation has been expired, it cannot be retained again. Because The Bible Said:

"TODAY IF YE WILL HEAR MY VOICE, HARDEN NOT YOUR HEARTS".

God Is Always Seeking for those who will Accept Him TODAY not Tomorrow. Accept God in THE NOW, not in the Later, because Later means it is too LATE for you.

Let us finally have a look at The Topic that is given. To understand fully The Pathway of A Child of God; this Pathway and Journey is A Testimony that has to be Revealed by A Child of God that is walking The Journey of The Christian's Pathway. This Pathway and Track is not like any other road surfaces, it is not like the High Way that many drivers would rather to drive on and go up to a speed of 110 KM; it must not even be compared to the road that we use when we travel in the Towns, that are filled with Traffic lights and bumper to bumper confusion. No, this Christian's Pathway and Journey is something that is very Unique and Dangerous, and cannot be compared to any other Journey.

But if it must have a comparison, it is best to describe this Christian's Pathway with The Movie that is Called Pearl Harbor or some other World War Movie. And in many cases at least Pearl Harbor and the World War had an ending, it had a Time that there was Peace Treaty being signed; it had the conditions that men were able to now go back home to their families and start all over again; it had a Season that at least a person could sleep in their bed and enjoy a night sleep, watch your family grow and enjoy the welcoming of the future Generations.

I say again NO, NO, NO; it cannot be Compared! This Christian's Pathway and Journey is completely different, because if it is that you're Destined to make it into God's Kingdom, Every Second of the Day must be A Mission to remain FOCUSED for the sake of your Soul, for the sake of the Soul of your family and for the Benefit of The Ministry. If you Fall asleep on this Journey outside The Watchful Eyes of Christ, you will die. The Christian's Pathway and Journey has to be travelled on with Extreme Caution, because there is a lot of Surprises; there is a lot of Unexpected Tunnels in the road, therefore moving too fast is not recommended. This road has Unexpected Speed Bumps and don't forget Rough Hill with Razor Sharp Stone. After being now Alert of the Fire, the Swords, the Serpent of Confusion, Principalities and Powers, Witchcraft and Sorcerers; The Child of God Must Remain Focused throughout the Season of the spirit of Doubt and Envy, that will be sown by someone you weren't expecting it from.

I say again No, it can never be compared; because for every Believer that is walking this Journey, the Conditions may be different; but when it all comes together it Reveals The True Christian's Journey; making known to all, that this is A Journey that must be Feared. Is must be Feared, but what is it that keeps The True Christian going? This is THE ULTIMATE REWARD OF ETERNAL REST WITH THE FATHER ABOVE.

From my personal experience, I can make known to those who

are reading this Message, to let you know that it is a Life Changing Experience. If for some reason a person decides to walk the Pathway of A Christian, and you're not Fully Persuaded, then I would advise you to think again; because every Challenge and Paths of direction has on The Journey An UNFORGIVEN FIRE, of which its main purpose is to Burn and Kill that which we love Physically, which is in complete contradiction to what is The Will of God for A Child of God Life.

THE MOUNTAINS

Determine Christians, which means Christ Like; those that has their Souls Planted in God are always desirous of the opportunity to Climb The Spiritual Ladder, but it must be noted that this Ladder of Spirituality Calls for The Appetite and The Spirit of God to be and to become Patient. Because while it is that we will seek to Climb as quick as possible The Spiritual Ladder, we must also remember that a Mountain goes up and requires a lot more energy than that of a person that is walking on a level surface. The Lord Reveals that every Spiritual Anointing comes with its own Personal Sacrifice for the person that is willing to SURRENDER a Physical Attraction. What this means is that the Higher A Child of God Choose to Climb in The Spiritual, it means that there will be A Greater Level of Discipline that is Required from that Child of God to be able to Attain that Spiritual Approval.

It was John The Baptist that revealed in The Scripture that Says: "CHRIST MUST INCREASE, BUT I MUST DECREASE".

It's the same thing for those who are seeking to Climb to A Higher Level in God; more of The Spiritual and less of the Physical. It also means that as we Climb The Spiritual Mountain, because the Physical is no longer being entertained, it therefore means that the appetite to do what was customarily for us to do, will no longer be in our atmosphere to force us to do, what is in contradiction to what

The Spirit of God Would have you now to do at the level to which you have Disciplined yourself to Climb into Spirituality.

The Beauty about The Mountain of Spirituality is that the person who seeks to Climb, is the same person that is of The Characteristics that they are Hungry to Receive of The Higher Level. Every Higher Level of Spiritual Authority in God that A Child of God Climbed to Receive; that Authority Remains with that Child of God, and it cannot be taken away, because that Child of God have done The Sanctify to Perfect The Sacrifice, which Allows The Heavenly Father to Release The Higher Level of Authority in God upon such A Servant. This Higher Level of Authority remains in The Lineage of that Child of God, for all their Generation that are willing to exercise the Discipline to Serve The Father with a Clean hands and a Pour Heart.

A Child of God need also to understand that The Mountain Experience and Authority cannot coexist with the Physical Attractions, because each Level of Spiritual Authority that A Child of God Climbs Will Reveal The Hunger of A Spiritual Appetite that is needed to Feed the Now Active Spiritual Man to Walk in The Authority that now Exist; what this means is that if there is no feeding of this Spiritual Man's Appetite then there can be no Approval to Walk in that type of Authority. Therefore, it is proven that many that have experienced The Mountain Top Level, and do not do what it takes to Feed or to keep Sharpen The Spirit Man; that man even though he had received The Experience of A Higher Level, will now find himself becoming Dull and less Effective in The Authority that God Has Already Imparted on him.

The Lord Always Warn me concerning His Blessing and Divine Approval:

"TO RECEIVE THE BLESSING OR THE ANOINTING IS ONE LEVEL; IT NOW REQUIRES AN HIGHER LEVEL THAN THAT WHICH YOU RECEIVED AT FIRST TO BE ABLE TO KEEP THAT SAME BLESSING".

There is A Scripture that Reveals that we must STIR UP The Gifts within us. In Fact what The Word of The Lord would have us to Understand is that The Gifts for The Approval and Authority of

The Higher Level is already in us; this is for those that have received of that Gift and Authority; but because we have lost Focused to Feed The Greater Authority in us, The Gifts remain but they are in a State of Dormant and not Active to Work.

Hosea Chapter 4:6.

"MY PEOPLE ARE DESTROYED FOR LACK OF KNOWLEDGE: BECAUSE THOU HAST REJECTED KNOWLEDGE, I WILL ALSO REJECT THEE, THAT THOU SHALT BE NO PRIEST TO ME: SEEING THOU HAST FORGOTTEN THE LAW OF THY GOD, I WILL ALSO FORGET THY CHILDREN"!

VALLEYS

This is an Experience many of us that are Christians wishes we could escape, but the truth is, there can never be a Mountain Top Anointing if there is not first a Valley Experience. I was speaking to someone the other day, and I said to that person that I give thanks to everyone and every condition that allows me to be in the experience of a Valley. Because if The Children of God do not understand the Purpose and the Special reason for The Valley, then it will certainly be identified that we will not have obtained the Materials or the Ingredience, the Stamina needed to endure The Journey to Climb The Mountain of Spiritual Elevation. Each Valley that is Destined for A Child of God to walk is brought forth for the main purpose being only to Teach that Child of God The True Strength of God's Foundation in them; because if A Child of God does not know The Foundation of The Almighty God, that Child of God Religion or Christian walk will become VAIN.

In The Valley Experience A Child of God Stop looking towards the help of man, because even if they desire to seek the assistance of man's help, it will not be Granted, because The Season and Time Dictates that this is The Time and Season for The Valley in your life. A Child of God will in The Valley's Journey soon realize that their only Friend is The Word of God. And no matter how hard you try to find another friend to help you along The Journey in this Experience of life, the conditions of The Valley will only force you back to The Words of God; because its only in The Word of God Can The True Strength be found to Allow A Child of God to Climb out of The Valley that they are experiencing.

Because The Valley is The Foundation of God's Word; after this Experience of The Valley, A Child of God will Mature to become Spiritually Strong, with all The Ingredience needed to Climb The Spiritual Mountain of God's Divine Approval and Authority. The Valley Season mainly depends on how long A Child of God chooses to not understand what is Required for them to learn what it is that they need and must learn from The Experience of The Valley. Because unless we learn The Lesson in The Valley, The Season of The Valley will continue until we have Learnt.

It basically means that if you're in The Valley Season and have not found The Word of God to be your only Friend, and Surrender to The Will of God's Word; then that Child of God will be spending a long time in that Valley Season because that Child of God Lacks Understanding. There is a lot of Christians that have not yet Matured; being Ignorant of what they should be doing, and that lack of Understanding causes us to be a long time in The Valley or in The Dark.

The Valley Experience if it is not embraced by the individual that is going through, to find out what it is that they need to Learn, in order to Adapt or Adjust or to be Born into A New Revelation of The Word of God; then The Atmosphere and The Environment of such an Experience will cause that person to suffer Spiritual Barrenness. This means that all types of Spiritual breakthrough will be withheld, until that Child of God Has Learnt The Valuable Lesson of being in The Valley to know that God Comes First.

On the other hand, many times The Valley is fixed to facilitate The Accepted Time of God's Perfect Timing, because each Child of God that has a Purpose in God, also has a perfect timing for their purpose to be fulfilled, but this perfect timing of God's Order, still cannot come to fulfillment unless that Child of God Has Received of the Ingredient that is required for that Child of God to Advance.

It is also realized in The Bible: Joseph got A Vision, and in The Vision it was Revealed to him that he was going to become the head for his family; however, that Destiny required that Joseph needed The Valley Experience, because if he is to lead for God, it basically means that he had to first become Knowledgeable of God and His Word. Because when Patiphar's wife choose to seduce Joseph, there was Revealed in Joseph The Foundation of The Standard of God's Word that could not be Shaken. Genesis Chapter 39:7-12. So it must be found in us, The Foundation of The Valley Experience, which is The Word of God Almighty, it must now become a part of who we are.

It must be Noted: In The Valley the Physical man dies, which therefore brings forth the Birth for The Spiritual Man; in The Valley all Children of God will learn completely what the World is all about; meaning we will all identify the True face of man that is under the influence of the spirit of the World.

In The Valley's Lesson, we will become well Knowledgeable, in that we will be able to identify spirits of different characters, and know without a doubt, who it is now that should be entertained within The Circle that The Lord Have Now Created for us to now Climb The Spiritual Ladder of Spiritual Maturity and Growth. It is a Fact that there will be those who will desire to become a part of our Circle once we have passed The Valley's Experience; but there is always a Reminder and a Scare that is Imprinted on The Souls of those who have been in their Valley, that as soon as there is something or someone that comes close to remind us of The Valley's Characters and spirits, because we have now Overcome and Elevated from that Experience, our desires will no more be conform to entertain the characters and spirits of that which we have out grown.

Every Child of God that has A Destiny for Ministry and The Kingdom of God, has their Personal Valley that they must Embrace in order for The Revelations of God's Word to be Manifested in that person. The Valley Experience can be compared to that of The Wilderness that Jesus Christ had to be a part of, in order to Become

The True and Full Manifestation of The Word of God; to overcome Principalities and Powers at The Highest Level. Therefore, those who are Shying away from The Valley Experience, think again, because it is in the Contract of each Child of God to become Sons of God; it's in The Valley The True Strength of A Child of God is realized. Truth be told, the Physical man is always going to shy away from the journey of the Valley, because the Physical man senses that death is eminent for its characteristics.

STORMS AND SEAS

St Matthew Chapter 7:24-27.

"THEREFORE WHOSOEVER HEARETH THESE SAYINGS OF MINE, AND DOETH THEM, I WILL LIKEN HIM UNTO A WISE MAN, WHICH BUILT HIS HOUSE UPON A ROCK: AND THE RAIN DESCENDED, AND THE FLOODS CAME, AND THE WINDS BLEW, AND BEAT UPON THAT HOUSE; AND IT FELL NOT: FOR IT WAS FOUNDED UPON A ROCK. AND EVERYONE THAT HEARETH THESE SAYINGS OF MINE, AND DOETH THEM NOT, SHALL BE LIKEN UNTO A FOOLISH MAN, WHICH BUILT HIS HOUSE UPON THE SAND: AND THE RAIN DESCENDED, AND THE FLOODS CAME, AND THE WINDS BLEW, AND BEAT UPON THAT HOUSE; AND IT FELL: AND GREAT WAS THE FALL OF IT".

I would ask My Readers to analyze for themselves very careful that within The Teachings of Jesus Christ, both men being Wise and Foolish were face and presented with the same Teachings; it went on to explain that one set of individual will choose to ACCEPT that which is being taught and also BELIEVE TO WALK IN IT. Now because this WISE set of people have now open their Hearts and Minds to The Teaching of The Word of God, there was found an immediate preparation to make certain that The Foundation of their Soul was Firm in God.

The other man or the other set of people also heard The Teachings, but they did not Believe. It is found to be Proof in this Scripture that when a person have not Accepted The Word of God to Believe in The Word of God, that person or persons will also choose to build for themselves upon the foundation of what they indeed believe in; in this case, what they will be building on for the rest of the their lives is in Fact Sinking Sand.

The True demonstration of this Message is to Identify and to show Proof to the Manifestation of those who are Building on The Solid Rock which is Jesus Christ from those who have established their beliefs upon those things that will never have a Foundation.

It must also be recognized that there was one event that remains constant, for the person that Believes in The Word of God and for the person that believes not in The Word of God; there is no doubt, that which remains constant is the True Fact, there is going to be A TERRIBLE UNFORGIVEN STORM. It doesn't matter how well and how sure the Foundation of the Soul is in God, this will not cancel the effects or the appointed time of The Storm and Sea.

In other words, The Storm and Sea for each person upon the face of the Earth whether you're Saved or not Saved, Believe or don't Believe, Wise or Foolish; The Storm and Sea is already FIXED for a Specific Time and Season within your life, and nothing can change it. Everyone must come face to face with THE STORM AND SEA. And there is no one that can outsmart The Storm and Sea. You can never plan above The Storm and Sea; and even all the preparation that is made for The Storm and Sea will still not be Effective or Enough, because The Storm and Sea is coming to make certain that every person have a ROOT of Foundation in The Word of God. By the time The Storm and Sea Passes, the only thing that will remain is the Root that is still Connected with the Foundation which is Jesus Christ The Word of God. A Child of God Storm and Sea will have different Faces, meaning no one's challenge is the same. There are some Believers that will face The Storms and Sea of Sickness, others will face Death. Some will face Financial Struggles on every side.

The Storm and Sea is Violent and Deep, it Shows no Mercy and it is certain, it Respects no one. The Bishops or The Priests of The Church is going to face The Storm and Sea, likewise The Pastors and The Ministers and Missionaries, Deacons, Overseers and Elders, Evangelists, Preachers and Teachers, Brothers and Sisters and don't forget those that are playing Church. I said this Storm and Sea is for everyone, therefore the Sinners will have the Front Seat.

A Believer that goes to all the Fasting Services, this will not stop or slow down the effects of The Storm and Sea; doing Prayer meeting in its Fullness will not weaken The Storm and Sea. Knowing The Bible till you reach to a Level that you can rehearse The Words, this will still not stop The Storm and Sea. Living the Life that is Required by God for A Christian's Journey, not even this, will Cause God to Redirect the pathway of The Spirit of The Storm and Sea for our Lives.

The Storm and Sea must now be recognize as a part of our Destiny. We will not live without facing The Storm and Sea; and it is certain, we will not die unless we've gone through The Storm and Sea, even if that's the very Storm and Sea that kills us; we would still have to face it. But after The Storm and Sea has Passed, there will now be a Calm; A Child of God will be Confident to know that not even The Greatest Force on Earth was able to shift The Love of God for His People.

FIRE AND WATER

There are Transitions that are needed for Every Child of God that is walking The Christian's Journey. And those Transitions will never be implemented by our own will and desires; which means that if God was to Reveal exactly what it was, and when it was that we will encounter A Difficult Valley or a Painful Mountain to climb, with giving us all the details of The Journey; I testify to all who read this Message, that we would not even move a Step on this Journey.

But GOD IS WISE, and GOD IS LOVE; Wise in that, He already Knows that because when we have started this Journey we are just Babes; The Lord Knows that there is a Procedure and a certain Process to go through while you're dealing with Babies; it takes time to Feed, it takes time to Nurture and to ensure that such A Child Grows. God Is Love, in that The Lord Knows that The True Position and Purpose for The Sons of God is to Stand UPRIGHT before God, and whatever it will take for God to Reshape A Child of God to The Likeness that Reflects His Glory, that is what is going to be carried out and fulfilled within the life of each and every Child of God that is Destined for The Kingdom of Heaven, and it is certain, we cannot Escape the Burning of THE FIRE and the Drowning of THE WATER, because God's Will for our lives must be Carried Out.

As for the time it will take for God to Establish Full Change within A Child of God life; this is totally in The Hands of God and also the Willfulness and the Obedience of His Children to Trust God enough to know that whatever God is Doing in our Lives, even if we are not able to physically see the finish line, we would have identified by Faith that there is a SURE END for all the Transformation that will take place within the life of A Child of God.

Truth be told, I am still young in the Faith in comparison to those who are well Seasoned. But this I can say so far: The Fire of Change BURNS and the Water of Change Drowns to KILL the Physical man.

The Bible Declares in The Book of Psalms 24:3-5.

"WHO SHALL ASCEND INTO THE HILL OF THE LORD? OR WHO SHALL STAND IN HIS HOLY PLACE? HE THAT HATH CLEAN HANDS, AND A PURE HEART; WHO HATH NOT LIFTED UP HIS SOUL UNTO VANITY, NOR SWORN DECEITFULLY. HE SHALL RECEIVE THE BLESSING FROM THE LORD, AND RIGHTEOUSNESS FROM THE GOD OF HIS SALVATION".

It must always be recognized that The Requirements of God throughout all Generation and Dispensation, is that of HOLINESS. Holiness is The Ultimate Standard; and God Has on this Christian's Journey, a Pathway that Shapes His People to Reflect His Requirements. Being a Christian we can forget about being given a chance when it is that we make a mistake in the eyes of other people; even if we have done something in secret, and it is our belief that we think that no one will know about what we have done; if it is that we are Destined for The Kingdom of God, then we can all be assured, that someone is going to find out about what we have done, because God's Requirement is that of CHANGE.

And if it Takes God to Use someone by giving that person the Understanding of what we have done wrong in secret, in order for that person to Humiliate us, to allow us to feel very bad, then that is what God Will DO, because His Requirements is always for our lives to Change from the Old Man and Transform into The Characteristics of The New Man. If it is that such a person that is Serving God realizes that they can sin and not be Reproached or Reproved for the sin that they have done openly or in secret; then that person should worry, because that person may have found themselves to be in the category that they are only CALLED but not CHOSEN.

The Bible Said in The Book of Proverbs Chapter 3:11&12.

"MY SON, DESPISE NOT THE CHASTENING OF THE LORD; NEITHER BE WEARY OF HIS CORRECTION: FOR WHOM THE LORD LOVETH HE CORRECTETH; EVEN AS A FATHER THE SON IN WHOM HE DELIGHTETH".

Now when it is that God Has Identified that The Characteristics of The New Man is now in full Effect; being now UPRIGHT before God, that's the Time that The Lord will now Manifest to Command these Words to fulfill in A Son of God life, according to Psalms 2:7-9.

"I WILL DECLARE THE DECREE: THE LORD HATH SAID UNTO ME, THOU ART MY SON; THIS DAY HAVE I BEGOTTEN THEE. ASK OF ME, AND I SHALL GIVE THEE THE HEATHEN FOR THINE INHERITANCE, AND THE UTTERMOST PARTS OF THE EARTH FOR THY POSSESSION. THOU SHALT BREAK THEM WITH A ROD OF IRON; THOU SHALT DASH THEM IN PIECES LIKE A POTTER'S VESSEL".

I Hope this Message would have been of Benefit to all those who have read. To God Be All The Glory and Praise; Great and Mighty Things He Has Done. From The Ministry of The Church of Jesus Christ Fellowship Savannah Cross Ltd. I remain your Friend and Brother; Pastor Lerone Dinnall.

CLIMB YOUR MOUNTAINS;
LEARN FROM YOUR
VALLEYS; ENDURE YOUR
STORMS AND SEA; ACCEPT
THE BURNING OF THE
FIRE AND THE DROWNING
OF THE WATER BECAUSE
HEAVEN IS OUR HOME.

Spend Your Time Seeking To Get To That Better Home

Message # 25   **Written in the year 2015.**

St. John Chapter 14:1-3.

"Let not your hearts be troubled: Ye believe in God, believe also in me. In my Father's house are many mansions: if it were not so, I would have told you. I Go to Prepare a place for you. And if I Go and Prepare a place for you, I Will Come Again, and Receive you unto Myself; that where I Am, there ye may be also".

I Give Honour to The Almighty God, I take this privilege to greet all My Fathers Children in The Name of Jesus Christ. Glad am I no stranger here, I take pleasure in God, to be writing another wonderful Message for God's People that will ensure that we are on the right path toward getting to Heaven.

In that Great Getting Up Morning, I will be there; The personal Question to ask ourselves is:

"WILL I BE THERE"? _____.

As the song writer says: Heaven, Heaven, Heaven is the place I want to be; I wonder within myself, is this only a song or does it carry meaning for us being A Child of The King. We've got to follow The Advise that God Gave to His People which says let a man examine himself that ye come not to condemnation. 1 Corinthians Chapter 11:27-31.

Many Topics and Messages that are written by me, I must confess that they are truly experience of my own life; as you live in this life you learn to appreciate and accept what God Is Actually Teaching you from the experience that you're going through. It is important for a person to know that the lessons in our lives is the experience that we would have endured and sometime fail to pass the Test. Another important detail in life is to know that this life that we are living in is A Test that God Has Given to us to See if we are disciple enough to endure the pressures of this life to pass The Test to make it into God's Kingdom. Without The Test there will definitely be no reward of receiving Heaven.

Think about it, Heaven Is Were God Is, and one of the main Characteristics of God is the fact that He Is Holy; God Himself Made it very clear in many of The Scriptures, in making His People know that He Is Holy and must not be compared to anything else on Earth or in Heaven. Leviticus Chapter 11:44-45. Now if God Is Holy, that simple means that The Dwelling Place where God Is must also Be Holy, therefore making us know that for us to get to Heaven, we've got to Train our Mind, Spirit and Soul to get to the place that we've become Disciple enough to reach THE QUALIFIED STATE of Being Holy. Holiness for us as Children of God to get to Heaven is A MUST, and not a maybe; we have to reach that mark, or else there is no way we are going to be where God Is.

God Gives unto His People The Commandment, The Requirements and The Guidelines for us to make it into Heaven; Many of us spend a lot of time and energy going around what God Ask us to Do, and rather doing the opposite of that which is Required of us to Do. And if we should ask ourselves this question:

"Is it our belief that there is A God and that there is A Heaven"?

The answer will return like a flood out of our mouths, by saying yes, there is A God, and Heaven Does Exist. Just speaking the words out of our mouth, don't actually makes it real for us. What makes it real is when we as Children of God Are Purposed, Focused and Disciplined to read The Bible and to make sure that we do exactly what The Bible Ask us to Do. We have to Train our Minds to be so Focused that we ensure that we do exactly what God Ask us to Do; considering that The Bible Said in Hebrews Chapter 10:36. Which Says:

"That we have need of patience that after we have done The Will of God, we might receive the promise".

It makes me ask this Question every time I read that passage of Scripture.

"Can I do The Will of God and still find myself short where His Requirement is concern"?_____.

This is a Question that we should all be asking ourselves; and when we have done that, then we will come to the conclusion that it is important for God's People to do The Will of God and to ensure that in everything that we are measured up to His Requirements; without this, there is no surety of receiving Heaven, The Dwelling Place of The Most High. The Bible Is Obviously Telling us that it is indeed possible for a person to do The Will of God in one part of there life and still come up short were God Requirements are concern to enter Heaven.

I have A Testimony concerning this passage of the Message; this is My Testimony:

"About two years ago, this being in the year 2013 in the month November to December, I applied to the Canadian Embassy for a Visitor's Visa so that I could visit my wife as she was due to have our child and was accepted to study in that country, I was

APPROVED FOR THE VISA. TO MY UNDERSTANDING I THOUGH I DID ALL THAT WAS REQUIRED OF ME TO TRAVEL, ONLY TO LEARN THAT WHEN I REACHED THE BOARDER IN TORONTO THAT THEY HAD ISSUES WITH ME, BECAUSE I CARRIED WITH ME EDUCATION CERTIFICATES AND DIPLOMAS. THIS TO ME SOUNDS, LOOK, AND IS STUPID; BUT FOR CANADIAN IMMIGRATION RULES OR REQUIREMENTS, THIS EVIDENCE SUGGEST TO THEM THAT I WAS ENTERING THE COUNTRY FOR THE PURPOSE OF WORK AND ALSO TO STUDY. THEY CANCELLED MY VISA AND SENT ME BACK HOME THE NEXT DAY. IT WAS AN HORRIBLE EXPERIENCE FOR ME; ONE THAT I PUT A LOT OF TIME AND PLANNING INTO AND NOT TO MENTION MONEY; BUT GOING THROUGH THIS EXPERIENCE MADE ME MORE STRONGER SPIRITUALLY AND WISER, TO REALIZE THAT THE BIBLE IS CORRECT, YOU CAN DO THE WILL, BUT HAVE NOT DONE EVERYTHING THAT IS REQUIRED OF YOU TO DO".

Having Learnt from my mistakes of Canada, I can now apply this experience with my development and my training of knowing God's Word to get to Heaven that I make sure that as I seek to know God's Will, I must also seek to make sure that I Do all that is Required of me from God to make it into Heaven. I'm also reminded in The Bible in The Book of 2 Chronicles Chapter 25:2. That there was a king named Amaziah of which The Bible Said that He did everything that was right in The Sight of God, but not with a perfect heart. Now this is the same Question that were asking in the previous statement:

"HOW CAN YOU DO EVERYTHING RIGHT IN THE SIGHT OF GOD, AND IT IS STILL NOT PERFECT"?_____.

The Bible Says it is so, who am I to say otherwise. Look at this, The Bible Said that he did that which was Right to Please God, and we are talking about God; and even though he please God, is service was not considered perfect. Now I understand when The Bible Said in St Matthew Chapter 5:48. Which Says:

"BE YE THEREFORE PERFECT, EVEN AS YOUR FATHER WHICH IS IN HEAVEN IS PERFECT".

Jesus Christ Showed to us what The Requirement of God Is, and that is for every man to be Disciplined, that we would reached the Goal of becoming Perfect in The Eyes of God, and not to be only right.

There are difference with the words Righteousness, Justified and Perfect. And this is the difference:

➤ Righteousness has a level and rule that is limited to the earth where man is concern, this is level 1, the first step of getting God's Attention; while we seek to get righteous it is mainly demonstrated and acknowledge by our own peers, and also seen from The Eyes of God as that person making one (1) step closer to come to Him.

➤ Justified is the next level, this speaks towards not just being Righteous, but being Upright in The Sight of God. What this means is that our righteousness that we possess have now exceeded the level of man's righteousness, therefore meaning, that not because man says or has proven or command that this is right, means that it is right in The Eyes of God; and we have realized and decide to please God rather than man.

➤ Being Perfect is the next level, let me say this, it takes time for a believer to become perfect in The Eyes of God; one of the main Ingredience for being Perfect is The Holy Ghost.

There are many people that will make you know that the speech of being perfect is but just a speech and nothing else, they will tell us that it doesn't exist. But where I stand is with The Bible, if The Word of God Says that we must be perfect, it basically means that God Has Given unto us The Potential for it to happen, because God Cannot Lie. I know for myself that I'm not perfect, but am I going to use that as an excuse, No!

The Lord Reveals to me that one of the most important thing in A Christians life is to be Disciplined to that which God's Word Ask of us to Become; If we don't Train our Mind, Spirit and Body to that which The Word of God Says, we will never be Able to do and to be

Perfect in that which God Requires of us to Do, thus resulting in us not being able to Enter The Kingdom of Heaven. There are parts of our lives that are already perfect, but God need for us to get every part of our lives in agreement to that which The Word of God Ask us to Do.

How many of us reading this Message, is actually spending the amount of time that we need to be spending, to ensure that when this life is over, we will be just in time to enter Heaven? This is a Message that is asking me the writer to ensure that I examine myself to see what my priorities are where Heaven is concern. Getting to Heaven I now know is a Big Thing; in fact, it is the Biggest and Most Important Mission for every Child of God that is serious about entering Heaven.

I find myself lately in my walking, in talking, in my deeds and also in my thoughts; carefully considering if everything is being done the way God Required it to be done. I'm also reminded by this song writer that says:

"IF YOU'RE LATE FOR HEAVEN, THEN YOU'RE JUST IN TIME FOR HELL".

Another song writer wrote that:

"YOU HAVE TO GO THROUGH HELL IN ORDER TO GET TO HEAVEN".

This makes me ask this Question: What am I willing to give up, willing to bear, to ensure that I enter The Kingdom of Heaven. Because when we have really considered this life and the pleasures of it, we would then ask ourselves the Question; is it really worth it. The Bible Warns that we should love not the World, neither the things that are in the World; it also said that the World passeth away and the lust thereof; which speaks towards everything in this life being Vain, only a show and just for a limited time. 1 John Chapter 2:15-17. Do I need to spend my time running after the glory of this World, when Solomon who was the wises king that ever lived, told us in The Book of Ecclesiastes Chapter 12:13. Which Says:

"LET US HEAR THE CONCLUSION OF THE WHOLE MATTER:

FEAR GOD AND KEEP HIS COMMANDMENTS: FOR THIS IS THE WHOLE DUTY OF MAN".

Here is an exercise that I would like us to try every day; Ask yourself this question from this day onwards:

"IS THAT WHICH I'M DOING, IS IT WORTH MY TIME FOR ME TO ENTER THE KINGDOM OF GOD"? _____.

This Answer will make us more aware and a lot more conscious about our day to day activities, to ensure that we spend it Pleasing God, and at the same time making progress to Enter Heaven. Each time I repeat this phrase I get to realize that there are a lot of requirements that are involved; but when you look on it at another angle; there is but just one requirement which is to Obey God's Commandment.

Let me share A Story with My Readers to show how important it is for us to do everything in our power to make it into Heaven. In St Luke Chapter 18:18-30. There was a certain Ruler that heard about Jesus, and believed that He was Sent from God; This Ruler saw the importance within himself to ask Jesus what would be The Requirement for him now, at the stage of his life at present for him to Inherit Eternal Life! And I must say that I really love this story. Jesus, after He had carefully Examined the Ruler, Told him that he must sell all that he had and give it to the poor; this request was overwhelming to the Ruler, because The Bible Declared that he was very rich and had great possessions.

There is one main thing that I realize in The Story, and this is it; the rich young Ruler asked to inherit or had a great desire to inherit Eternal life; but upon asking a request like that, he never really understood what exactly is Eternal Life. Eternal Life is A Gift of Spiritual Life to live with God Forever; Now if this is so, why then did the rich young Ruler never understood that everything that he Possessed in this life would never really be able to allow him to enter that Eternal Life that he so earnestly desired to inherit.

This is what The Lord Needs us to Realize; to receive Heaven we must first deny ourselves the luxury of this life, in order for us to receive a home that is completely Spiritual. God Loves us and wants the Best for us at all times, but do we love ourselves? _____. To express the truth, when I read The Bible and it Explained to me The Beauty and Wonders of Heaven; and especially being A Child of God; I can only say that I find myself falling in love with Heaven. Revelations Chapter 21&22.

We've got to realize that this Earth is just A Test for us to Inherit Heaven; whether we will Pass The Test or Fail The Test, it really depends on us; because God Gives unto every man the same equal opportunity to Inherit Heaven; He Gives unto all man a Privilege that is called FREE WILL. Which means we choose what will become of our own Destiny; Right or Wrong, Heaven or Hell, God or the devil; CHOOSE!

Here are a list of Tools that the Soul will have to use in order for us to make it into God's Kingdom, they are as follows:

- Pain
- Sufferings
- Disappointments
- Troubles on every side
- Principalities and Powers
- Sorrows
- And The People of God must get ready for even Death

If we have not made up our Minds to go through these Test; then it will be that we are not truly ready to endure all, to receive A Gift from God that is completely Priceless, and just imagine this, The Bible Says that we will be walking on Streets of Pure Gold. Wow! God is so Rich that what we consider to be our most valuable treasure, that's the same material that God Will Use for us to walk on it in His Kingdom. Wow!

I Hope this Message was helpful for your journey to make it into God's Kingdom. All Praise and Honor Be Directed to The

Almighty and Most Holy God. From the Servant of God; Pastor
Lerone Dinnall.

WORK FOR THAT BETTER
HOME IN THE NAME
OF JESUS CHRIST.

THE WALLS OF DIFFICULTIES

Message # 75　　　　　　　**Date Started August 4, 2017**
　　　　　　　　　　　　　　　Date Finalized August 4, 2017.

GREETINGS IN THE MIGHTY Name of Jesus Christ Our Soon Coming King, it is a Privilege for me to be in this Position that I can be an Available Vessel for God to write Inspiring Messages for God's People. In this life that we live, there will become times when it is necessary for A Child of God to receive a word of Inspiration that will no doubt Aid in the development of our Christian Walk. And I hope very much that these Messages have done just that, which is to fill the Gap and Creases of our Minds that have not yet began to receive of The Light of God.

The Walls Of Difficulties, this expression is in no way foreign to those of us who are reading this Message; as it is, that all People of all Language and Culture have experience what it feels like to be presented with Walls; and then have to be in that position that we must climb those Walls; then to endure the period of time that is Set and Fixed for those Walls to remain as a stumbling Block in our lives.

Now when it is seen that by the duration of Climbing these Walls, something now begins to change, in that we begin to think that there is no way that these Walls could get any Worse; it is then by the snap of the finger that the Walls have now elevated to a Level that it is now not only a Wall or Walls but now have become a Difficult Wall or Walls. It is at this time we begin to ask ourselves the Question:

"What is this or is this Fair"?_____.

The Lord Has Revealed that Knowledge is a Key component in the Life of A Child of God, because without the Spirit and Gift of Knowledge A Child of God will Forever be in a State of Confusion as to what must be the road for that Child of God to walk on. The Lord Has Revealed that for everything there is A Foundation to that which A Child of God has to Endure for their Walls of Difficulties, and that Foundation stems from The Seed of ENVY that Adam and Eve had allowed, that caused for their Souls to Disobey The Living Word of God.

Now because of The Seed of Envy which is the Main Seed that Births all type of Sin, of which we as Children of God were Born in a Generation and Generations and Lifetime upon Lifetime of perfect Practice to Commit Sins. This Yoke of Sin even though for those of us which have given our Lives to God by water Baptism, and then the Infilling of The Holy Ghost, this Yoke is not yet fully released by these actions or life transformation, but it is a Fact that unless we as Children of God are Fully determined to pursue A Walk of Holiness and Righteousness, it will be observed that this Yoke and Seed of Envy will no Doubt have remained and still have a big impact on our lives as Christians.

The Lord Has Revealed that because there are many evidence of Sin that still remains in the life of A Child of God; there is A Spiritual Screening that is placed within the Life of each Child of God to Allow that Child of God to be Fully Transformed in The Likeness of The Requirements of God's Will, and that Spiritual Screening is known as every Walls of Difficulties that we face, of which it's only purpose is to Burn Off or to Kill each Character in us that does not represents or reassembles The Character of The Living God.

The Truth and Fact is, that God in His Complete Manifestation cannot be Mixed with any forms of Sin; therefore, the more we esteem to become of The Likeness of God, it's the more that we will be required to endure more and more Walls of Difficulties which is The Spiritual Screening of God's Will, to ensure that we become exactly what The Likeness of God Represents.

Here is one thing we may hear a lot of while seeking to Grow in The Church and in The Spirit of God:

"WE MUST DROP OFF IN ORDER TO PUT ON".

The Bible Declares that John the Baptist Said:

"HE MUST INCREASE, BUT I MUST DECREASE". St John Chapter 3:30.

That's the exact same thing that The Lord Is Asking His Children to Fulfill. This however takes some time, depending on the Soil of The Child of God and their determination to become Discipline to every Will and Requirements of The Heavenly Father. We may wonder at times why is it that we spend so much time enduring one Wall of Difficulties that we face. The answer to that question is because we have not yet learned what it is that we need to learn from the Wall of Difficulty that we face, in order for us to know exactly what it is that we need to Drop Off or to Kill from our lives that doesn't Resembles The Character of The Living God.

This example shows the Expression as to why it is that every Christian has a Different Wall of Difficulty to Climb. It is because that, what one Child of God may have as a Difficulty overcoming, the other Child of God would have already Conquered that Wall of Difficulty to know what it is that they must Drop Off in order to Put On of The Likeness Of God. This however does not exempt any Child of God from another Wall of Difficulty; because we all must learn by Now that God's Requirements are so High, that it is certain that there will always be Walls of Difficulty for us to endure in order for us to even try to measure up to The Requirements of God. But Measuring Up we must, if it is that we are to Inherit The Kingdom Of God.

There is Seen in The Eyes of The Lord A Child of God that has surpass the Wall of Difficulty to allow them to Steal, and it is also Observed by The Eyes of God that same Child of God have not yet pass the Wall of Difficulty which causes that Child of God to tell a Lie. And while one aspect of that Child of God is Now Perfect, in that under no condition and Test of Life that Child of God will never take something that does not belong to them, of which those spirits that allows Souls to steal cannot and will no longer affect that Child of God.

On the other hand of that Child of God life, the spirits to tell a Lie are still being entertained, thus these spirits to tell a Lie causes the Defense of God's Spiritual Screening to be Activated, thus causing a Wall of Difficulty to be Present at all times in the life of that Child of God until that Child of God have learned to Conquer those spirits that causes them to tell a lie.

Every Walls of Difficulty that we face is associated with movements of the spirits that causes that Wall to be Enforced by God; therefore, it must now be a Clear Knowledge that it's not a Man that causes our Walls of Difficulties, it is a Fact that it is our Character that is Managed by the spirits of the Seed of Envy that causes God to Bring Forth that Wall of Difficulty.

It must also be understood that with every Walls of Difficulties that we have Overcome by the Discipline of The Holy Ghost, there will be Birth in our Lives A Divine Blessing from The Father Above.

I Will Bless The Lord at all Times, May His Praises Continue to be in My Mouth. I Hope this Message Has Helped God's Children, May God Continue to Bless our Lives in The Direction of His Likeness. Continue to Pray for this Ministry. Pastor Lerone Dinnall.

OUR WALLS OF DIFFICULTIES CAN BE CONQUERED THROUGH OBEDIENCE OF GOD'S WORD.

NOTHING IS WRONG IF WE CRY OR BECOME FRUSTRATED DURING THE TEST; OUR MAIN JOB IS TO FINISH THE TEST...

Message # 50　　　　　**Date Started August 19, 2017**
　　　　　　　　　　　　　Date Finalized August 19, 2017.

LET ALL THE PEOPLE of God Honour, Magnify and offer Praise to The Only Living God; Jesus Christ The Saviour of Mankind. Glad am I no stranger to The Trials that A Child of God Should and Must endure in order to Become The Sons of God. Happy am I to be of Inspiration that I can write Messages for God's Chosen People, and I said Chosen People because not everyone will find or see these Messages or others Messages from other Saints important to read; because The Chosen of The Lord must now come to realize that The Tithes of God is what it is, that being HOLY; and not only speak to those who offer Money or Time or Talent, but The Tithes of The Lord mainly speak to those who have fashioned their lives to Pattern The Walk of Holiness; and as many there is that have come to the Understanding that Holiness Is A Must in order to Inherit The Kingdom of God.

There will also be the Knowledge in such A Saint to be of the Understanding that those who are Holy Indeed Represent The Tithes of Saint for the Land unto God; and if indeed we have found ourselves Representing The Tithes of The Lord, then we can Rest knowing that what we have to endure, at the end of all that will happen, it will manifest that we have obtained our Final Resting Place.

St Matthew Chapter 26:36-46.

"THEN COMETH JESUS WITH THEM UNTO A PLACE CALLED GETHSEMANE, AND SAITH UNTO THE DISCIPLES, SIT YE HERE, WHILE I GO AND PRAY YONDER. AND HE TOOK WITH HIM PETER AND THE TWO SONS OF ZEBEDEE, AND BEGAN TO BE SORROWFUL AND VERY HEAVY. THEN SAITH HE UNTO THEM, MY SOUL IS EXCEEDING SORROWFUL, EVEN UNTO DEATH: TARRY YE HERE, AND WATCH WITH ME. AND HE WENT A LITTLE FURTHER, AND FELL ON HIS FACE, AND PRAYED, SAYING, O MY FATHER, IF IT BE POSSIBLE, LET THIS CUP PASS FROM ME: NEVERTHELESS NOT AS I WILL, BUT AS THOU WILT. AND HE COMETH UNTO THE DISCIPLES, AND FINDETH THEM ASLEEP, AND SAITH UNTO PETER, WHAT, COULD YE NOT WATCH WITH ME ONE HOUR? WATCH AND PRAY, THAT YE ENTER NOT INTO TEMPTATION: THE SPIRIT INDEED IS WILLING, BUT THE FLESH IS WEAK. HE WENT AWAY AGAIN THE SECOND TIME, AND PRAYED, SAYING, O MY FATHER, IF THIS CUP MAY NOT PASS AWAY FROM ME, EXCEPT I DRINK IT, THY WILL BE DONE. AND HE CAME AND FOUND THEM ASLEEP AGAIN: FOR THEIR EYES WERE HEAVY. AND HE LEFT THEM, AND WENT AWAY AGAIN, AND PRAYED THE THIRD TIME, SAYING THE SAME WORDS. THEN COMETH HE TO HIS DISCIPLES, AND SAITH UNTO THEM, SLEEP ON NOW, AND TAKE YOUR REST: BEHOLD, THE HOUR IS AT HAND, AND THE SON OF MAN IS BETRAYED INTO THE HANDS

OF SINNERS. RISE, LET US BE GOING: BEHOLD, HE IS AT HAND THAT DOTH BETRAY ME".

St Matthew Chapter 27:45-50.

"NOW FROM THE SIXTH HOUR THERE WAS DARKNESS OVER ALL THE LAND UNTO THE NINTH HOUR. AND ABOUT THE NINTH HOUR JESUS CRIED WITH A LOUD VOICE, SAYING, ELI, ELI, LAMASABACHTHANI? THAT IS TO SAY, MY GOD, MY GOD, WHY HAST THOU FORSAKEN ME? SOME OF THEM THAT STOOD THERE, WHEN THEY HEARD THAT, SAID, THIS MAN CALLETH FOR ELIAS. AND STRAIGHTWAY ONE OF THEM RAN, AND TOOK A SPUNGE, AND FILLED IT WITH VINEGAR, AND PUT IT ON A REED, AND GAVE HIM TO DRINK. THE REST SAID, LET BE, LET US SEE WHETHER ELIAS WILL COME TO SAVE HIM. JESUS, WHEN HE HAD CRIED AGAIN WITH A LOUD VOICE, YIELDED UP THE GHOST".

There is one True Fact for those of us who are Children of The Most High God, and that Common Understanding is for us to be Knowledgeable that this life is only our TESTING GROUND; a lifetime of Trials and Test in order for us to earn the rights to obtain that which is an Everlasting Life with our Saviour. It all comes back to the Foundation Value that God Has Fixed from the Foundation of the World; and that Foundational Value for all Mankind is known as FREE WILL.

God's Genius Spirit / Mind at work, in order to Manifest that which is Light from Darkness and Righteousness from Unrighteousness; of which God Has Not Put a label on any persons that should be born into this life, even though He Knows the outcome of each Soul that walks the face of this life; God Still Insist that the way forward to Erect Proper Judgment, to Establish His Kingdom is to Allow each Soul to choose for themselves the road in which they must travel on, with making sure that each person has gotten their fair share of knowing what is the Right Path, the Straight and Narrow way that will lead to Life Eternal.

Jesus Christ The Manifestation of God to Mankind from The Hands of God, Paved The Pathway for an example to all Mankind to

Show that it is indeed Possible for all man through the Knowledge of The Most High God to be able to Live Above Sin by The Birth of The Spirit of God in Man. This Spiritual Rebirth is The Living Conscience of God in Man, which Amplifies a man Natural abilities, to that of The Abilities of God in portions to enable a common man to become The Anointing Spirit of The Most High God, just as it was seen and Manifested in the life of our Saviour Jesus Christ.

Then many ask the Question:

"WHY IS IT THAT EVERYTHING MUST BE DONE IN THE NAME OF THE LORD JESUS CHRIST"? _____.

Answer:

"JESUS CHRIST IS THE FULL MANIFESTATION OF GOD TO MAN, THE SECOND ADAM, WHICH HAS PROVEN THAT HE BOTH CONQUERED DEATH AND HELL, AND RISEN A COMPLETE SPIRITUAL MAN TO LAY DOWN THE EXAMPLE FOR ALL TO FOLLOW IN HIS FOOTSTEPS BY LIVING OUR LIVES ACCORDING TO THE PRINCIPLE AND GUIDELINES THAT HE FOLLOWED, WE WILL ALSO BE ABLE TO BE VICTORIOUS, BECAUSE THE SAME SPIRIT THAT WAS MANIFESTED IN JESUS CHRIST, IT IS THE SAME SPIRIT THAT IS MANIFESTING IN US, IF IT IS THAT WE HAVE RECEIVED OF THE CLEAN SPIRIT".

I made mention of The Clean Spirit because we must Understand by now that not all spirit is The Clean Spirit, The True Undiluted Holy Ghost that only God Can Give. Now for those of us that are desirous to understand The True Holy Ghost, Clean Spirit; I would ask you to follow the Example that The Lord Jesus Christ have Laid out for us to Observe. Which is to Try the spirits to see if they are of God or of man or of devils. And it doesn't matter how long it takes for a person to make sure that they are sure; this is needed because each person must know the type of people that they allow to circulate in their Circle.

Because if it is found that there is in your Circle those spirit that are not of God, then it is a Fact, that those spirits with their type of Influence will seek to Overpower The True Spirit of God that is in You. Therefore, it is asked by each Child of God to make sure that they try and try again to make certain that those who are directly involved in your Circle are those that have Manifested The True Holy Ghost, Clean Spirit of God.

True Holy Ghost Saints are those who seek to Live Up to The Requirements of God and keep Improving to Elevate in The Will of God. This does not mean that those who have Received of The True Holy Ghost, Clean Spirit are those who will never make mistakes; but rather they are observed by the Attitude and the Character that Manifest in them a Godly Sorrow of Repentance to ensure that what caused them to slip will not happen again. Therefore, because Repentance is a constant reminder and lifestyle of a person that have Received of The True Clean Spirit of God; this person is found often BURNING THE SACRIFICE which Manifestation is the Tears of The Saints, not done to put on a show; but is rather Manifested because that person have experienced The Forgiving Touch of God's Hand, that let that person know that their Father which Rules Heaven and Earth Has Forgiven them of their Sins.

Therefore, it is found and identified by The Spirit of God, that those who have Repented, and those who continue to Repent, are those who have illustrated The True Manifestation of The True Holy Ghost Clean Spirit of God.

NOTE: Repentance Main meaning is to Turn or to Change from doing a Sin which was customarily structured for a person to do, with the evidence of having A Godly Sorrow, that will ensure that such a person will never do again what they have now become ashamed of doing.

Therefore, when it is identified in The Church that there is a member that keeps making the same mistakes of committing a Sin; then we need not to wonder and ponder about their life, the Truth is being Revealed before our very eyes; that person whoever they may be, have not yet Repented of that one Sin; thus it is Manifested that they will keep on doing it, because they have not yet Received of The Clean Holy Ghost Spirit, that causes sin to be Burned from their Lives, which forces Repentance from our Souls.

It must however be Revealed that a life of A Child of God that have Received of The True Holy Ghost Clean Spirit, will reflect that Perfection to Do God's Will is not Achieved in One Day; but it is given unto us a Lifetime to be Born in The Characteristics of The Clean Spiritual Man; therefore, no one can point a finger to Judge because the same person that points a finger to judge is the same person that has some sin that they also need to Repent of. The Manifestation is the KEY; just keep on watching the Manifestation, and it must be Revealed in time those who are The Clean Holy Ghost Saints, from those who are The Pretenders of the Faith.

The Lord Jesus Christ, His Life as an Example Showed to us that there will become times in our lives that we will become Frustrated; His Life Proved that there are going to be times when there is no one around that we can depend on, not even to offer a word of Prayer ; His Life also Proved to us that we are destined to walk in a path that the Flesh must die in order for The Spirit Man to live; His Life Proved that there will be times when it seems that The Face of God Is Nowhere to Be Seen; and at that time, The Life of Jesus Christ Proved to us that in spite of all that we have done for God, there will be fulfilled the time that this Flesh will Cry.

The Life of Jesus Christ Proved that there is found on this pathway those who will and must Abuse us; Persecute us; Beat us; Spit in our face, Whip us and also Slap us; there will be found those who will Refuse to give us water, but instead choose to give to us Vinegar and Gall; meaning that we will never receive that which we truly deserve from man; there will be those who will also use the Sword to pierce our side, and use their mouths to kill our Souls.

The Life of Jesus Christ Reveals that no matter how much good we do; the Flesh which is the Physical man will always Vote and Shout for a known Sinner to live than for The Righteous to Survive. It is also realized that the Life of Jesus Christ Manifested that He Conquered Death and Hell, and has All Power in Heaven and on Earth, had obtain The Key of Death and Hell through His Death; therefore, we must Understand that if we are purposed to Finish each Test, we will also become Victorious over all the Elements and spirits of the World, and at the end to see our Saviour with A Smiling Face and not as A Frowning Judge.

Nothing is wrong if we Cry or become Frustrated during The Test, our main Job is to make sure that we Finish each Test. Children of God, go ahead and Cry; Cry and keep on Crying; because Tears is a Language that only God Understand. Cry and keep on Crying, because all those Tears has A Vial in Heaven with your name written on it; and when it is full, not even the Devil in Hell can stop your Victory, therefore Cry, because Jesus Christ was The Full Manifestation of God, and He Also Cried to Give to us an Example to know that it is OK for A Child of God to CRY.

And speaking about Crying, it is Important to Understand that God Is Seeking for this CRY:

C: Conscious :- Are we of the Full Understanding of what brings us to the point that we will now pour out our Hearts to God, or is it just another Show.

R: Repenting :- The only time that God Will Move with Compassion to Feel that which Burns our Heart, is when we have been born in the Understanding to become Knowledgeable that in order for God to Take us Serious, we have got to become Sorry for the wrongs which we have done; thus the Appetite is no longer alive to commit that same Sin.

Y: Yearn :- To have a Longing to feel, to experience The Touch of God's Hand when we have Cried, and that cry brings forth an immediate response from The Father Above; because He Recognizes that the Cry came from A Son of God, therefore, there must be an Answer to that Son from His Father.

This Type of Manifestation when we Cry is sure to Receive The Full Attention From God Above, which said:

"BEFORE YE CALL, I WILL ANSWER, AND WHILE YOU'RE YET SPEAKING, I WILL HEAR".

To God Be All The Glory, Great Things He Has Done. I Remain God's Faithful Servant, Continue to Pray for this Ministry, in The Mighty Name of Our Lord and Saviour Jesus Christ, The King of all kings and The Lord of all lords. From Pastor Lerone Dinnall.

NOTHING IS WRONG IF WE CRY OR BECOME FRUSTRATED DURING THE TEST, OUR MAIN JOB IS TO FINISH THE TEST.

STOPPING THE CRY!

Message # 97   **Date Started June 1, 2018**
                                     Date Finalized June 4, 2018.

LET ME FIRST DECLARE that All Glory, Honor and Praise goes to The Father of Heaven and Earth, Jesus Christ The Lamb of God. I Greet all My Father's Children in The Wonderful Matchless Name of Jesus Christ our Soon Coming King.

It was brought to My Understanding by The Unlimited Mind of God, A Great Disease that has been caused to grow and to multiply in Society, Countries, Nations and Languages, by Manipulating Especially God's People in a Conduct which will now see God's People Changing their Focus of Dependency from God to that which the World has put into Systems that Governs our everyday activities.

I am reminded of the speech of The Late Bishop Austin Whitfield, when he spoke to us in Sunday School, to allow us to Understand that the Devil is the smartest being that A Christian will ever come across not considering The Power of The Almighty God. There are many that distinguish the devil as being a fool or stupid, but The Mind of God Has Allowed me to Understand that the devil and the influence of the devil's action must be one that is carefully observed and understood by a person that is seeking to walk The Way of The Lord.

The Actions and Influence of the devil has been in study for generation on top of generations, leading back to the conspiracy that took place in Heaven for one such person by the name of Lucifer, desiring The Kingdom and The Glory of The Almighty God. It is no doubt that the master of deception has now perfected his craft, and has now become 100% Effective in everything he now seeks to manipulate.

It was Revealed to me by The Manifestation of The God Head, when it is that I decided to seek knowledge for activities of the World, to try to understand the Mysteries of that which is being perfected within the Minds of the sons of man for generations. One of the first thing I Questioned The Lord for His Intelligence to Reveal, was the number one Question that would be asked by any Christian, and that Question was:

"LORD, WHY IS IT THAT THERE IS SUCH A LONG DELAY FOR YOU TO BRING FORTH DELIVERANCE FOR YOUR PEOPLE"?

The Lord Response to me Was:

"MY PEOPLE HAS STOP CRYING OUT TO ME FOR DELIVERANCE, THEREFORE THE VESSEL THAT SHOULD BE FILLING UP WITH THE CRY AND REQUEST OF MY PEOPLE IS EMPTY, THUS MY PEOPLE ARE SATISFIED WITH THE CONDITIONS THAT THEY HAVE FOUND THEMSELVES IN; THEREFORE, DELIVERANCE IS DELAYED UNTIL MY PEOPLE BEGINS AGAIN TO CRY OUT TO THE LORD FOR THEIR DELIVERANCE".

WOW!

The Lord Allowed me to search The Scriptures, for in The Scriptures there is Eternal life for God's People. I discovered in The Book of Genesis Chapter 21:17-21, after Abraham took the Advice of his wife which was later confirmed by The Voice of God, to send Hagar and his son Ishmael away; The Bible Made Mention that the mother placed Ishmael a distance from herself, and she began to cry;

The Bible then Said that the Lad which was Ishmael began to cry, and The Lord Heard the cry of the Lad from Heaven.

It is Amazing to see and to discover The Power of A Child of Inheritance; because The Bible Clearly Allowed for us to understand that the Mother which was Hagar, she was crying, but then The Bible Placed the event in a Category by itself for the Child that came from Abraham, which was Ishmael; The Bible Said, The Lad Cried, and The Lord Heard the Cry of the Lad from Heaven, and gave an Immediate Response. It is understood that The Lord Spoke to the Mother on behalf of the Child, reason being, the boy Ishmael was still a child, therefore, he could not understand how to hear from God, much less to speak back to God. But the Revelation of this Scripture Reveals that God Is Inching to Hear The Cry of The Righteous Generation.

I went further in My Study, and I Observed in The Book of Exodus Chapter one to Chapter three that in order for God to Prepare Moses for The Destiny that he was to fulfill, there had to be A Cry made by The Children of Israel for the Burdens that their Taskmasters place them under, to fulfill harsh requirements through the Councils and Government of the land of Egypt.

Let's have a look at what The Bible Said about The Cry that was made to God. Exodus Chapter 2:23-25.

"AND IT CAME TO PASS IN THE PROCESS OF TIME, THAT THE KING OF EGYPT DIED: AND THE CHILDREN OF ISRAEL SIGHED BY REASON OF THE BONDAGE, AND THEY CRIED, AND THEIR CRY CAME UP UNTO GOD BY REASON OF THE BONDAGE. AND GOD HEARD THEIR GROANING, AND GOD REMEMBERED HIS COVENANT WITH ABRAHAM, WITH ISAAC, AND WITH JACOB. AND GOD LOOKED UPON THE CHILDREN OF ISRAEL, AND GOD HAD RESPECT UNTO THEM".

Further information was observed when I looked in The Book of Esther Chapter 4. In previous Chapters it explains in summary that Haman was appointed to rule over all the officers and princes and people of the Land, this gave Haman High Authority over the kingdom. It is reported that when Haman walked by the kings gate it was given as command for all to bow before Haman and reverence him; this was not carried out by Mordecai, therefore, when it was told Haman what Mordecai did, this angered Haman to the point that he decided that he was going to have Mordecai and all the tribe of Israel be destroyed in one day, this was approved by the king.

The Decree or law that was signed went in this order, Esther Chapter 3:8-13.

"AND HAMAN SAID UNTO KING AHASUERUS, THERE IS A CERTAIN PEOPLE SCATTERED ABOARD AND DISPERSED AMONG THE PEOPLE IN ALL THE PROVINCES OF THY KINGDOM; AND THEIR LAWS ARE DIVERSE FROM ALL PEOPLE; NEITHER KEEP THEY THE KING'S LAWS: THEREFORE IT IS NOT FOR THE KING'S PROFIT TO SUFFER THEM. IF IT PLEASE THE KING, LET IT BE WRITTEN THAT THEY MAY BE DESTROYED: AND I WILL PAY TEN THOUSAND TALENTS OF SILVER TO THE HANDS OF THOSE THAT HAVE THE CHARGE OF THE BUSINESS, TO BRING IT INTO THE KING'S TREASURIES. AND THE KING TOOK HIS RING FROM HIS HAND, AND GAVE IT UNTO HAMAN THE SON OF HAMMEDATHA THE AGAGITE, THE JEWS ENEMY.

AND THE KING SAID UNTO HAMAN, THE SILVER IS GIVEN TO THEE, THE PEOPLE ALSO, TO DO WITH THEM AS IT SEEMETH GOOD TO THEE. THEN WERE THE KING'S SCRIBES CALLED ON THE THIRTEENTH DAY OF THE FIRST MONTH, AND THERE WAS WRITTEN ACCORDING TO ALL THAT HAMAN HAD COMMANDED UNTO THE KING'S LIEUTENANTS, AND TO THE GOVERNORS THAT WERE OVER EVERY PROVINCE ACCORDING TO THE WRITING THEREOF, AND TO EVERY PEOPLE AFTER THEIR LANGUAGE; IN THE NAME OF KING AHASUERUS WAS IT WRITTEN, AND SEALED WITH THE KING'S RING. AND THE LETTERS WERE SENT BY POSTS INTO ALL THE KING'S PROVINCES, TO DESTROY, TO KILL, AND TO CAUSE TO PERISH, ALL JEWS, BOTH YOUNG AND OLD, LITTLE CHILDREN AND WOMEN, IN ONE DAY, EVEN UPON THE THIRTEENTH DAY OF THE TWELFTH MONTH, WHICH IS THE MONTH ADAR, AND TO TAKE THE SPOIL OF THEM FOR A PREY".

Now we can Imagine what took place when Mordecai and the Jews heard what was to come to pass; but the Question is this:

Did not God Know that this was going to take place in the life of Mordecai and the Jews? _____

_____.

It has been Revealed to me by The Spirit of God, that everything that takes place within the lives of God's People, it is done for one purpose only, and that is to Bring forth A CRY from the lips of God People, which will then Manifest God's Divine Glory, which will only be for Himself and not to give Honour to any other being. In a Nut Shell, Our Father Loves to Show Off for His Children in a Big Way, that all can Observe and take Notice as to which set of People Belongs to The Living God.

Therefore, the next Question to ask is this:

Does God Enjoy when His People CRY? _____

_____.

It's not a Sense or Understanding for God to Enjoy when His People Suffers that causes them to Cry, but rather The Word of God Gives us the Understanding to become Knowledgeable of the clear Fact, that God Requires for His People at all times to be and remain Dependable on The Movements of The Will of God.

FACT: God Is Always and will always remain to be A Jealous God; meaning that, God Requires all the Attention from His People, and is found to be at all times Upset with His People whenever it is that His People are placing all their attention on that which God Has Created. We've become so adapted to worship the Creation instead of Worshipping THE CREATOR. And all the time when we do this, it's clear evidence that God's People finds themselves in Bondages that causes us to Cry when it is that we have decided and come to the Understanding that we need now to Cry out to God for Help.

Getting back to The Book of Esther Chapter 4:1-3.

"WHEN MORDECAI PERCEIVED ALL THAT WAS DONE, MORDECAI RENT HIS CLOTHES, AND PUT ON SACKCLOTH WITH ASHES, AND WENT OUT INTO THE MIDST OF THE CITY, AND

CRIED WITH A LOUD AND BITTER CRY; AND CAME EVEN BEFORE THE KING'S GATE: FOR NONE MIGHT ENTER INTO THE KING'S GATE CLOTHED WITH SACKCLOTH. AND IN EVERY PROVINCE, WHITHERSOEVER THE KING'S COMMANDMENT AND HIS DECREE CAME, THERE WAS GREAT MOURNING AMONG THE JEWS, AND FASTING, AND WEEPING, AND WAILING; AND MANY LAY IN SACKCLOTH AND ASHES".

It was understood that because The People of God Cried, and Queen Esther also Fasted and Cried out to God; God Heard The Cry of His People; God Brought forth Deliverance in A Unique manner, that no one could expect. Because there was A Sincere Cry from God's People, of which they were not satisfy with their Conditions and Future, this type of Prayer with A Cry, Moved God to Remember His Covenant Which He First Made with Abraham, Isaac and Israel, and also for all those who will Keep His Commandments and walk in His Precepts. This Cry from The Children of Inheritance will no doubt Cement the future Destiny of God's People upon the Land, because it is written:

"THE RIGHTEOUS SHALL INHERIT THE EARTH".

But The Righteous need to Cry to God for their Deliverance.

The Topic Says: Stopping The Cry. The Influence and Actions of the Devil has now received the Master's Certificate, Diploma and Ph.D. of knowing exactly What to do; When to do; How to do what he in intends to do, Who exactly to use, to cause God's People at times to be distracted away from Crying out to God for Deliverance. We've become so Blinded through this world's Glamor and Fashions, that we have not yet understood that all this is done to cause us to lose our way of following after Christ Jesus.

I would ask God's People to analyze for themselves, if the following statements is True.

➢ Have we not discovered that our Cry is being Stopped?

_____.

➤ Have we not notice that we just can't find enough time anymore to be in Relationship with God?
_____ .

➤ Have we not notice that our time for Rest with God, within His House is being restricted by even our employers, who have now picked up the practice to ask us to make ourselves available on the day of Worship to be at work? _____ .

➤ Have we not realized that we cannot find the time anymore to be in a Day of meaningful Fasting with God, which will no doubt build our Relationship with God? _____ .

➤ Have we not seen that there is less family time for you and your children? _____ .

➤ Have we not seen that Sickness has taken over the Land, and our Healer is no longer Prayer that works with sincere Fasting, but instead our new healer is the Doctors and Physicians of which some of them don't believe in The God that Can Heal? _____ .

➤ Have we not notice that every time the Government of the day issues a new law to further oppress the lives of God's People, have we not seen that there is always some distractions of entertainment that causes us to lose focus on that which is made law to force not only us but our children to follow in a lifetime of Bondages? _____ .

➤ Have we not notice that The Cry of God's People Is Being Stopped! _____ .

All Praise, Glory and Honour goes to The Unlimited Mind of The

Universe, Jesus Christ The Lamb of God. From The Ministry of The Church of Jesus Christ Fellowship Savannah Cross Ltd. God Bless you. Pastor Lerone Dinnall.

ARE YOU A CHILD OF GOD?

IS YOUR CRY BEING STOPPED?

WHAT WILL YOU DO ABOUT IT?

"I COMMAND YOU THIS DAY TO BREAK FREE IN THE NAME OF JESUS CHRIST"!

LET US TAKE A
CLOSER LOOK

Message # 14   **Date Started June 30, 2016.**
                                      Date Finalized July 10, 2016.

GREETINGS FAMILY OF GOD; All Praise be unto The True Power of Jesus Christ. I take this opportunity to Salute All The Wonderful People of God. It is indeed a great privilege that I'm in a position like this to be speaking on another Topic that The Lord Has Inspired. Here we have a Topic with a strange Message; A Message that Says:

"LET US TAKE A CLOSER LOOK".

How many times, it is that we feel embarrassed; that someone had to show us what we are doing wrong? Not that there is something wrong with someone trying to correct us; but many times when we are corrected, we know within ourselves that this correction was something that we by ourselves should have seen; or maybe it is that we have said: No one sees and understand what I am doing, therefore, it is not a problem for me.

Thinking like this and acknowledging that we are thinking like this is a Major problem for our lives. This type of thinking shows that we are not seeking to Improve, but rather to remain on one level.

If your Serving God, and have not the desire to become A Better Christian; then I must tell you the truth; your Salvation is vain. There must always be the desire in us to reach to the other level.

Have we seen in The Bible how The Word of God Speaks about Peter, that they laid the sick in the streets, on beds and on couches that the shadow of Peter might heal the sick. Act Chapter 5:15-16. That's a level that Peter Reached In God. People of God can I say; that's the Level we all can Reach In GOD.

The Bible Said Greater Works than these which He Has Done shall we be able to Do. But we are not doing The Greater Works, because we are satisfied with just being an ordinary Christian; not knowing that the word Christian does not speaks of a person being Ordinary but Special. We make ourselves Ordinary because we Settle.

This is what we do and say: Brother John and Sister Mary is Serving God in this fashion, therefore, nothing is wrong if I choose to Serve God at that same level.

The Bible Encourage us to take no man as an Example; but we must rather be An Example before others. God Is Real; therefore, His Expectation from us is also Real. The Bible Said that he that knoweth to do Good, and doeth it not, to him it is Sin. This person shall be beaten with many Stripes; but not only the person that knoweth to do Good; it is also made mentioned of the person that do not know what is wrong, and does that which is wrong; that person shall receive punishment; but with fewer stripes than the person that knoweth to do the right things and doeth it not.

I was looking at a program on the Television, when I heard the commentator made mention of the Seven Deadly Sins of The Bible; at first I was shocked, because I never knew that it was knowledgeable to that person. The Seven Deadly Sin the person was referring to, also known in The Bible to be the seven Abominations that The Lord Hates; this can be found in The Book of Proverbs Chapter 6:16-18. Which speaks of six of these sin God Hates; and the seventh one, from the group being an Abomination unto God which is seen in verse 19. They are as Follows:

1. A PROUD LOOK.
2. A LYING TONGUE.
3. HANDS THAT SHED INNOCENT BLOOD.
4. HEART THAT DEVISETH WICKED IMAGINATIONS.
5. FEET THAT BE SWIFT IN RUNNING TO MISCHIEF.
6. A FALSE WITNESS THAT SPEAKETH LIES.
7. ANYONE THAT SOWETH DISCORD AMONG BRETHREN.

The Word Discord Means:
TO BRING FORTH DISAGREEMENT; DIFFERENCE OF OPINION; STRIFE; DISPUTE AND WAR.

Anyone God Finds doing anything of this sort; their very prayer is an ABOMINATION. This allows me to realize that the Truth Is Revealed to everyone, but not everyone is choosing to do what is the Truth.

Let us take a closer look on our Christian life; to pinpoint exactly what this Message seeks to establish, let us take a look at the different functions of our spirit that makes us who we are; according to the decisions that we make.

1. THE SPIRIT TO MOVE ACCORDING TO GOD'S WILL
2. THE SPIRIT TO SEE, THAT GIVES US THE FREE WILL TO CHOOSE WHAT WE SEE
3. THE SPIRIT TO HEAR
4. THE SPIRIT TO TASTE
5. THE SPIRIT TO SMELL
6. THE SPIRIT TO FEEL
7. THE SPIRIT TO UNDERSTAND; THE SPIRIT TO BE KNOWLEDGEABLE; THE SPIRIT OF WISDOM, THESE SPIRIT IS THE MANIFESTATION OF THE GOD HEAD IN MEASUREMENT.

All these are given unto us by God, as abilities, for us to be able to use them to choose to do the right things, by a word that is called FREE WILL. These Abilities from God Are Amplified when it is that A Child of God Has Received The Gift of The Holy Ghost.

People of God, the time is winding down, if we do not start to show some interest in what we are doing in our members for God, then it is sad to say; that we won't be a part of The Marriage Supper. I know that these things are hard to say; but it is certainly true.

Is everything that were saying in accordance with God's Will? _____.

Is everything that were doing, is it Pleasing Our God; and most important, when we think; what do we think about, with the intention of doing what were now thinking; is that which were thinking and planning to do, is it an Abomination in The Eyes of God? _____.

These are Questions we need to ask ourselves; and if it is that we are in the wrong; then the time to get it right is definitely now. We have got to be careful of the time ahead; there is coming a time and a season that The Bible Says:

"HE THAT IS UNJUST, LET HIM BE UNJUST STILL: AND HE WHICH IS FILTHY, LET HIM BE FILTHY STILL: AND HE THAT IS RIGHTEOUS, LET HIM BE RIGHTEOUS STILL: AND HE THAT IS HOLY, LET HIM BE HOLY STILL". Revelation Chapter 22:11.

Daniel Chapter 12:9-10.

"AND HE SAID, GO THY WAY, DANIEL: FOR THE WORDS ARE CLOSED UP AND SEALED TILL THE TIME OF THE END. MANY SHALL BE PURIFIED, AND MADE WHITE, AND TRIED; BUT THE WICKED SHALL DO WICKEDLY: AND NONE OF THE WICKED SHALL UNDERSTAND; BUT THE WISE SHALL UNDERSTAND".

When this time and this season has arrived; then My friends, there is nothing we can do anymore about the condition that we find ourselves in. Because at that time there will be no more GRACE; no more MERCY; no more REPENTANCE; no more SALVATION.

The Bible Says in Hosea Chapter 10:12.

"SOW TO YOURSELVES IN RIGHTEOUSNESS, REAP IN MERCY;

BREAK UP YOUR FALLOW GROUND: FOR IT IS TIME TO SEEK THE LORD, TILL HE COME AND RAIN RIGHTEOUSNESS UPON YOU".

To add to that which The Word of God Is Saying; it is always a time and a season for us especially God's People to Seek The Lord. Isaiah Chapter 55:6. Says:

"SEEK YE THE LORD WHILE HE MAY BE FOUND, CALL YE UPON HIM WHILE HE IS NEAR".

The Fact of life that we all need to understand is that God is not always going to be Near; meaning that the opportunity won't always be available for us to Seek God to know about Him, thus allowing ourselves to come into Relationship with God; there is coming a time that even The Word of God; this Precious Word from Heaven will no longer be available for us to read.

Amos Chapter 8:11-12.

"BEHOLD, THE DAYS COME, SAITH THE LORD GOD, THAT I WILL SEND A FAMINE IN THE LAND, NOT A FAMINE OF BREAD, NOR A THIRST FOR WATER, BUT OF HEARING THE WORD OF THE LORD: AND THEY SHALL WANDER FROM SEA TO SEA, AND FROM THE NORTH EVEN TO THE EAST, THEY SHALL RUN TO AND FRO TO SEEK THE WORD OF THE LORD, AND SHALL NOT FIND IT".

There are many events that took place in the past where this action was Manifested, but we must believe that has we approach the end time of this life, that the effects of that which happened in the past will surely take place in the times ahead. Has it was in the Beginning so shall it be in The End.

Have a look on this Scripture; Zephaniah Chapter 2:1-3. In summary, this Scripture is asking for God's People to gather ourselves before the day of The Lord's Anger Come upon us. The Scripture went on to Say that we must Seek The Lord's Righteousness; Seek Meekness; we should do this Now; and store up for ourselves, that when The Day of The Lord Anger Is Come, we would be safe from all His Destructions.

Revelation Chapter. 22:14. Says:

"BLESSED ARE THEY THAT **DO** HIS COMMANDMENTS THAT

THEY MAY HAVE RIGHT TO THE TREE OF LIFE; AND MAY **ENTER** IN THROUGH THE GATES INTO THE CITY".

I specifically Bolded the word DO and the word ENTER; for us to realize that, except we all DO GOD'S WILL; there is no way we are going to ENTER GOD'S REST. It is time for us to look on ourselves; and say to ourselves that it's time to get Clean; and for those of us that have already considering ourselves to be clean; let us with Humility Remain Clean.

It is our Destiny to make it. Awake every morning; look in the mirror; and tell yourself that I have already made it. It's already DONE. Together we can; together we will; because we BELIEVE.

All Praise be unto The True Power of Jesus Christ. From the Servant of God; your Brother; your Friend; your Minister and Pastor Lerone Dinnall.

LET US TAKE A CLOSER LOOK; TAKE A MAGNIFYING GLASS LOOK ON OUR WALK WITH GOD.

THE KING'S WINE

Message # 28   **Date Started April 20, 2016.**
                                     Date Finalized April 23, 2016.

GREETING TO ALL GOD'S Wonderful People; I greet you all in The Matchless Name of Jesus Christ, Our Soon Coming King. Surely it is a privilege to be sharing with you another Wonderful Message Inspired by The Almighty God. I have a confession to make; while it is that I am writing these Messages to you; I'm also benefiting from the experience; therefore, don't think that you're the only one that is gaining from these Messages; because I find myself a lot of the times going back to look on these Messages to Be Inspired to see what God Has Instructed for His People to Become.

Here we have A Wonderful Topic, The King's Wine; to make it very clear to My Readers; The King that we are referring to, is none other than Our Lord and Saviour Jesus Christ. And The Wine that we are talking about; is you and me; The Servants of The Most High God. I saw it important to make that very clear, because I've seen people use words, and turn those words to their liking or their understanding.

The King's Wine; we all should know by now the importance of a King; even so much more the importance of our Lord and Saviour Jesus Christ. He Died that we should have life; we are all indebted to God for the rest of our Existence, and not only our lives, but for all our children and their children and for all mankind.

When we look to consider all these Facts; we may wonder within ourselves how is it, that there are still persons that do not care about offering unto God AN ACCEPTED SACRIFICE.

NOTE: It's not only when we come to Church that our Sacrifice is given to God, where the Pastor is present; where the Missionaries, Ministers and Saints can see us. It is important to know that we also offer the main Sacrifices in our Walking; in our Talking; in our Living, especially in Secret where no one can see us. The Bible Declares to us in The Book of Romans Chapter 12:1.

"I BESEECH YOU THEREFORE, BRETHREN, BY THE MERCIES OF GOD, THAT YE PRESENT YOUR BODIES A LIVING SACRIFICE, HOLY, ACCEPTABLE UNTO GOD, WHICH IS YOUR REASONABLE SERVICE".

Here we have Brother Paul, begging us that we should make sure that everything that we offer to God is Acceptable, especially that which is done in our bodies; making us know that it is our Reasonable Duty to Perform.

Let me use this opportunity to Reveal this little secret: Everything that we do for God; it is compared to that of Wine; being poured into a Glass for God to have as A Drink from His Children. Can you just imagine, an Unworthy Sacrifice trying to even come before God as an Offering for God to Drink! And I used the word trying, because anything Unworthy cannot come before God; much less to be poured out into a glass for Him to Drink.

So it is with us as Children of God, if we do not seek to Walk Uprightly; Talk Uprightly; Live Uprightly before God; then our Sacrifice will only be offered in Vain. The Bible Said in The Book of St John Chapter 15:2.

"EVERY BRANCH IN ME THAT BEARETH NOT FRUIT HE

TAKETH AWAY: AND EVERY BRANCH THAT BEARETH FRUIT, HE PURGETH IT, THAT IT MAY BRING FORTH MORE FRUIT".

This Scripture basically explain to us that God Needs us to give Good Sacrifice; and not only to give Good Sacrifice but to keep on getting better that we reach to a place that we can give Perfect Sacrifice.

There is a Story in The Bible that I would like to share with you; coming from The Book of Isaiah Chapter 5. The Lord Was Making comparison with us His People as being A Vineyard that He Has Planted; The Lord Explained that He Planted The Vineyard Himself, and He Made Sure that everything was done the correct way that it should have been Done. The Lord Showed His Disappointment by letting us know that when it was time for Him to Receive The Benefits of that which He Had Sown in a Perfect Manner; there came up from His Choice Vine, WILD GRAPES.

If you should do a research, you would get to realize that Wild Grapes was not desirable, because they were not Sweet. The Lord Called for Jerusalem, and men of Judah to judge; making us know that man who is unworthy to be judge, will also agree with Him in this matter; that they also could realize for themselves that the work that God Did, was indeed Perfect.

Therefore, how is it, In The Mind of God that I Have Sown Seeds In Good Soil; and Removed all evidence of harm that could have come nigh My Vineyard. I Gave the rain from Above; I Fenced in My Vineyard from every traps and plans of the enemy. The Lord's Question Is:

"WHY IS THIS SO"?

Further in The Scripture you can read for yourself The Punishment The Lord Carried out on His Chosen Vineyard. This story is making reference to us as Christian that God Have Sanctified and Cleansed us by The Blood Which He Shed on that Cruel Cross; when He Said:

"IT IS FINISHED; MAN'S REDEMPTION IS PAID".

Now after God Has Done so much for us in making sure that we are now free from sin; to walk in The Newness of life. Don't you see that it is a great injustice, and a lack of respect to The Mighty

God; when we as Christians do not live up to The Requirements of Offering to God The Sacrifice; The Wine that He Deserve from our Service.

We've got to start looking on The House of God as The Cup that The Wine Will Be Poured Into; and The Wine Is The True Sacrifice that comes from Chosen Worshipper. Whenever time we come to God, and are sure that we are Serving In Spirit and In Truth; then we can rest assured that The King Has Received A Worthy Pouring Out of Wine in His Glass, bringing forth A Smile on His Face instead of A Frown.

I Read A Story in The Bible, and compared it to this Message; the story is about Joseph in Genesis Chapter 40. This is where Joseph interpret the dreams of the Butler and that of the Baker. I'm not talking about the interpretation of the dreams; I'm more focusing on the injustice that was done to the king that cause them both to be cast into prison. It's not clear what these two men did exactly, because The Bible Did Not Make Mention of it. But it is definitely clear that an offence was carried out that cause the king to be displeased.

This is what we do know; the Baker must have been in charge of the preparation of all that the king should eat; The Butler, his job should contain that of making sure that he taste everything that comes before the king; to ensure that the taste is healthy, worthy to come before the king, and also to ensure that the king's wine is of the very best, and His glass is always full when it is the required time for Him to drink.

They both did something that caused them to be in prison; it may have been a small matter but an offence was made to the king. This is My Question; looking on the Topic, The King's Wine; how many of us take it upon ourselves to make sure that all the duty that we are required to do for God is Spotless, Worthy, Acceptable, and Perfect.

This story of the Butler and the Baker, should be an example for us. They both offended the king; but look on it; only one of them was forgiven of that offence. I know what you're going to say; You'll now say thank God for Mercy. Bishop Austin Whitfield Often Told Me:

"TRY NOT TO MAKE A MISTAKE WHEN IT COMES ON TO THE

ALMIGHTY GOD; BECAUSE MANY PEOPLE THAT LOST THEIR FIRST LOVE; WILL NEVER BE ABLE TO FIND IT BACK AGAIN; EVEN IF THEY COME BACK TO GOD; THE RELATIONSHIP WILL NOT BE THE SAME".

I took his advice; and I'm not a person that wants to find out if God Can Get Angry at me. We may not die when we make a mistake, because we are under GRACE; but it is certain from The Revelations that God Gave to me, that we lose a little more of God's Glory that we could have Received. This is why we have in The Church many members that are a part of The Church for years; and because they cannot find it within themselves to offer unto God True Sacrifice, they will continue to remain being a Brother, or a Sister, and never able to Climb The Spiritual ladder to Become A Minister; or A Pastor.

Moses found out the hard way when he was told to speak to The Rock; he Disobeyed and Struck the Rock instead; thus causing God to Not Let him Enter The Promise Land. Disobedience is the main word that is going to manifested in this Topic which causes us not to offer The True Sacrifice.

There was a Queen in The Bible, by the name of Vashti; Her Husband the king was having a feast of celebration for his kingdom; the king commanded his wife the Queen to come forth to show herself of her beauty before all the king's guest; Vashti the Queen refused to obey the king's command; thus resulting in a law being made to remove the Queen from her office, and to let someone else take her place.

Do you think this story has anything to do with The King's Wine? _____.

You better believe it does!

How many times we disobey a command; that was given by our Pastor to carry out, in The Service of The Lord! _____.

How many times we fail to do, what The Word of The Lord Asked for us to Fulfill! _____.

NOTE: This is very important; The King's Glass, is already Set to Receive of The Wine that is to be Poured out in it; if we are offering

Unworthy Sacrifice to God; it therefore means that our Sacrifice can never be The Wine that is going to fill The King's Glass. With that being said; The King's Glass has to be full for it to be Accepted.

Can we recall The Story of The Fig Tree; The Bible Said that it wasn't the season for Figs; but in The Eyes of God; it is viewed that when we are in Position to perform Service to The Master, we must always find ourselves ready to offer True Sacrifice. St Matthew Chapter 21:18-22.

Consider This: If we are Servants to God; what if God Decide to Awake us out of our sleep, to Perform a service of Prayer for someone. Is our Answer going to Reflect a Character that we Tell God that we are unable to do what He Asked us to Do because its now a period and time for sleeping! _____.

Therefore, if we cannot fill The King's Glass at that time in the Morning; it therefore means that The Lord Is Going to Find someone who Is Worthy to offer The Accepted Sacrifice that His Glass Will Be Filled with their Sacrifice.

Let's think now; where does that leave that person that refused to Obey What God Commanded? _____.

The Answer is REJECTION. God Will No Longer Put His Trust in that Vessel, that would see Him Depending on that person. Has it was seen that Queen Vashti was rejected, and her office was given to another; so will that Vessel Be Rejected; and the basic Task that God Asked that person to Fulfill, He Will Find someone who is more than willing to do the job that was asked to be fulfilled. To know more about Queen Vashti, The story can be found in The Book of Esther Chapter 1.

To compare something that went bad; to something that went good; this is what we will now look on. In The Book of Nehemiah Chapter 1. The Bible Declared that Nehemiah heard some bad news about the walls of Jerusalem being burnt and destroyed. After Fasting and Praying about the situation; and also asking God to Forgive the sin of His People and also his sin. Nehemiah being the king's Cupbearer; in other words, he was the king's Butler; went forth in the presence of the king to do His duty; never realized that it was an offence to be in the presence of the king with a sad countenance.

Howbeit because Nehemiah was a worthy servant; this offence did not caused him his life; instead it brought a concern to the lips of the king by asking him: Why is thy countenance sad? When Nehemiah began to tell the king what had befallen his home town, and also asked request that permission be granted him to return to Jerusalem to rebuild the walls of the city; and also that materials would be granted unto him for the use of rebuilding the walls of Jerusalem.

The king, because he knew the type of servant Nehemiah is, he quickly granted him all that he desired to have and also wished him a save travel. This Story is a reflection of what our Relationship can be like in God. If it is that we are A True Servant and Worshipper of God; that Reflects that God Can Always count on us to give to Him A Clean Refreshing Drink of Wine through our Sacrifice. Then, just has how Nehemiah was granted Great Favors from his master, so is it that we will be granted Great Favors from God Above, if we just Remain Being True Servants for God's Service.

I would like to share with My Readers another Testimony: I remember growing up in The Church; I would often hear My Bishop speak with me, to encourage me to stay with The Lord, and to do everything that I need to do for Him with A CLEAN HAND. He would often Say:

"JUST GIVE GOD A CLEAN WORK, IF YOU GIVE TO GOD A CLEAN WORK, NOTHING CAN HARM YOU"!

I took his advice to try my very best, to Serve God with my whole Heart; Might and Soul. I remember I was at Church one day Serving God; The Lord Used a Prophet to speak to me, and told me that He Was Going to Give me something that I didn't asked for; and it was going to be a Great Blessing. I wondered for a long while what that Blessing was; and still even now, I am still wondering if I have received that Blessing. But this is what I know: I went to My bed one Night and I heard A Voice Speaking to me in my sleep, telling me that I must seek a piece of land that I can build an Altar for God. I continued to hear The Voice Speaking to me at different times in My Visions, until I started hearing prophecies of the same Instructions.

I Obeyed, and went to meet with a person that I knew sold land; to my surprize before I went to meet with this man, The Lord Had Already Spoken to the man, and Instructed him concerning me of the piece of property on a hill that He Had Already Prepared for me to start a work for Him; that I could Worship Him there in Spirit and in Truth. The Lord even went as far as to show the man a picture of me. When I got to the man's house; he basically ran to me, and let me know that he got a vision of me from God concerning a piece of land that The Church will be Built On. Could you just imagine My Surprize! I was completely Blown Away. And knowing Who God Is, and What He Can Do; I'm still wondering if this is The Blessing He Spoke of, or is there more to come?

The King's Wine; Let's just meditate on it for a while. Do you realize that this Wine must be of The Highest Standard and Quality! Truly Special, and well Preserved. Now if we are Children of The Most High God, and our Sacrifice is considered to be the very Wine that The King Drinks; When we look on ourselves; here is the Question to Ask:

"DO I TRULY REPRESENT, TO EVEN BE IN THE SENTENCE OF SOMETHING THAT THE MOST HOLY GOD INDULGE IN"? _____.

When we all consider this Question carefully; then we will realize, how much more work that is needed for us to do; to really find ourselves measuring up to the standard; that our sacrifice can truly be that of The King's Wine.

Look at this: Not only are we The King's Wine; but we are even more known as The King's Bride! I can just imagine The Lord Using A Magnifying Glass on us, to make sure that He Searches all of us, to See if there is any Spots, and Wrinkles; any Dust and Dirt; anything that will cause our White Garment to Be Soiled or Spoiled; when it is that we are Worshipping.

We are reminded in The Scriptures and Songs, that **(99 & ½)** won't do; we've got to aim for the **100%** mark. We can't be pre-occupied with the fact that we are only going to Church to give The Sacrifice. We have got to reach a place that we realize that going to Church is just not good enough nor is it the only Requirement. Majority of A True Child of God life is that which they do outside of The Church. Everyone learn to be Discipline and even Pretend to be Truthful in Church; but when Church is over, and Pastor and all the other members are not watching us; that's where the True life and Sacrifice is.

If we cannot correct our True self; then we must surely know that there is no way we are going to be able to Give unto God A Sacrifice that will be Accepted to be The King's Wine.

I hope that you have learnt something from this Message; I Hope this Message was a Blessing to you. Let us My Fellow Brethren, keep the Fire Burning in us, and continue to lift up A Standard for God. Remember that only God Alone Knows the True you.

For The Matchless Name of Jesus Christ. From the Servant of God; Your Brother; your Friend; Your Minister; Your Pastor, Lerone Dinnall.

ARE YOU THE KING'S WINE?

THE DIFFERENCE BETWEEN GIVING UP TO THAT OF LETTING GO

Message # 73

Date Started June 23, 2017
Date Finalized June 23, 2017.

THERE IS NO GOD but Jehovah, There is no King but The Father of The Universe, There is no Saviour but Jesus Christ The Lamb of God; and the Big secret is: All The Manifestation of God, is equal to the same One God. I Honour, Praise and Exalt The Only High God, which made the Heavens, the Earth, Seas, Hills and Valleys; to Him Be Glorified, from Everlasting to Everlasting.

I am happy for this Topic, reason being, I believe that there are a lot of Christians that are troubled, because it is the belief that many associate having to lose, means that this event is a sign of Weakness. Now if we should observe what the word difference mean in the context of this Topic, we will identify that it means that there are some similarities in the event that took place, but somewhere in the process of what took place, there is a clear difference that it had opposite pathways. Meaning that many will use their eyes to bring forth Judgment; while those that are Children of The King will use The Spirit of God to Instruct them as to what is Righteous Judgment. Therefore, the life of A Child of God remains to be a Mystery to the World, because it Is God that Reveals Secrets to those who Fear Him.

Let's have a look on what it means to GIVE UP. Hebrews Chapter 10:35-39.

"CAST NOT AWAY THEREFORE YOUR CONFIDENCE, WHICH HATH GREAT RECOMPENCE OF REWARD. FOR YE HAVE NEED OF PATIENCE, THAT, AFTER YE HAVE DONE THE WILL OF GOD, YE MIGHT RECEIVE THE PROMISE. FOR YET A LITTLE WHILE, AND HE THAT SHALL COME WILL COME, AND WILL NOT TARRY. NOW THE JUST SHALL LIVE BY FAITH: BUT IF ANY MAN DRAW BACK, MY SOUL SHALL HAVE NO PLEASURE IN HIM. BUT WE ARE NOT OF THEM WHO DRAW BACK UNTO PERDITION; BUT OF THEM THAT BELIEVE TO THE SAVING OF THE SOUL".

It is clearly identified in The Scripture that Man's main consciousness is that of Choice, meaning Free Will. If any man draw back; meaning that such a person have seen the pathway, but then chooses not to walk in that way that he should walk in which leads to Eternal Life; and this action is known as Giving Up. In the same Scripture it gives also an example for those who will not Give Up, because God Has Planted The Seed of His Spirit, to ensure that such a person sees and foresees what will happen if they decide to Give Up, of which when they have seen the challenge of the path and the outcome, The True Worshippers will become more determined to make sure that there is not a spirit in us to Give Up.

Let us have a look at LETTING GO: Genesis Chapter 13:5-12.

"AND LOT ALSO, WHICH WENT WITH ABRAM, HAD FLOCKS, AND HERDS, AND TENTS. AND THE LAND WAS NOT ABLE TO BEAR THEM, THAT THEY MIGHT DWELL TOGETHER. AND THERE WAS A STRIFE BETWEEN THE HERDMEN OF ABRAM'S CATTLE AND THE HERDMEN OF LOT'S CATTLE: AND THE CANAANITE AND THE PERIZZITE DWELLED THEN IN THE LAND. AND ABRAM

SAID UNTO LOT, LET THERE BE NO STRIFE, I PRAY THEE,
BETWEEN ME AND THEE, AND BETWEEN MY HERDMEN AND THY
HERDMEN; FOR WE BE BRETHREN. IS NOT THE WHOLE LAND
BEFORE THEE? SEPARATE THYSELF, I PRAY THEE, FROM ME:
IF THOU WILL TAKE THE LEFT HAND, THEN I WILL GO TO THE
RIGHT; OR IF THOU DEPART TO THE RIGHT HAND, THEN I WILL
GO TO THE LEFT.

AND LOT LIFTED UP HIS EYES, AND BEHELD ALL THE
PLAIN OF JORDAN, THAT IT WAS WELL WATERED EVERY WHERE,
BEFORE THE LORD DESTROYED SODOM AND GOMORAH, EVEN
AS THE GARDEN OF THE LORD, LIKE THE LAND OF EGYPT,
AS THOU COMEST UNTO ZOAR. THEN LOT CHOSE HIM ALL
THE PLAIN OF JORDAN; AND LOT JOURNEYED EAST: AND
THEY SEPARATED THEMSELVES THE ONE FROM THE OTHER.
AND ABRAM DWELLED IN THE LAND OF CANAAN, AND LOT
DWELLED IN THE CITIES OF THE PLAIN, AND PITCHED HIS TENT
TOWARDS SODOM".

Now have a look at this, Abraham being the Uncle to his Nephew, asked his Nephew to choose, knowing according to custom and decency that he had all rights to decide and dictate who gets what, seeing that he was the Foundation of The Promise that God Had Given to him; a Promise that Lot was but just a follower to witness The Powerful Hands of God on his Uncle Abraham.

Have you ever been in a position that you know that you are right, and have all rights; but instead, it's like The Witness of The Holy Ghost Touched your Mind, to let you know that God Sees and Understand, therefore, we need not to worry because The God of Heaven and Earth Will and Can Always Make A New Way which will still lead us to our Destiny. This was the position that Abraham found himself in. I can just imagine Abraham being in that Position, heard The Voice of God Saying to him:

"REMEMBER I SAID TO YOU, WHOSOEVER BLESS YOU, I
WILL BLESS THEM; AND UNTO HIM THAT CURSES YOU, I WILL
CURSE HIM".

Abraham was of the Attitude that many of us would look on as being a foolish Attitude; but in Abraham's eye, he had proven more than once that God Is Almighty. Therefore, Abraham showed us the true meaning and The Foundation of what it takes for A Child of God to Trust God enough that they can LET GO of what they and the World thinks that they have to hold on to.

To show you how the World and how Flesh looks on things; Lot being the Nephew of Abraham, it never even came into his understanding to accept that if there is going to be any choosing, it should have been Abraham his Uncle, The Man of God, be given the first fruit of choosing what part of the land he would desire. Lot didn't even realized that Abraham his Uncle was not blessed by man's mouth, but by God's Mouth; which means that even though he choose what seemed to be at that time the better part of the land, because The Bible Said that the land could be compared to The Garden of The Lord; Lot was soon to find out that even if he choose what seemed to be the best land; because of God's Promise upon the life of Abraham, even if Abraham was in the Valley, that Valley would then become The Blessing from The Lord.

Therefore, the Good land that Lot thought he had inherited; because of The Promise that was placed on Abraham's Life, that land could not be maintained as the best and most blessed of lands, because the soul of Abraham was not dwelling in that land, therefore, the land had to Become A Curse.

And to let us understand even clearer; Lot could not even hold unto the land that he choose, because God Never Made him A Promise to possess much less to inherit that land. God's Covenant Promise was made between Him and Abraham; therefore, when the Testing and the Storms of life arise; only Abraham was found upon The Foundation of The Word of God; therefore, only Abraham could Stand and Remain in The Promise of God.

But have a look at this: The Bible Said that Lot Lifted up his eyes, and beheld the plains of Jordan. That word LIFTED UP, can be compared to the Desire and Intentions, the Expectation of Lot; being the Nephew of Abraham, the person which is The Foundation of God's Blessing for His People; Lot really and truly thought that he could and would become Greater than Abraham; that was the reason why his soul choose the better land.

This is also a comparison of what happen to Lucifer; he thought with all his Mind and Soul, that he could become greater than God. This Example should bear witness to all Saints that are True Worshippers. Whatever God Has Placed and Fixed for your Inheritance and Blessing, as long as you remain Faithful to God, even if someone chooses to do something better than you, that which they have done cannot change God's Mind regarding your Inheritance, because it is FIXED.

And each Child of God needs to understand that if we are Truly Serving God, then we need not to Envy others for their Blessing from God, because God Has Not Ran out of Inheritance for His People. And learn something about Letting Go; if Abraham did not let go of his rights to dictate terms, he would have found himself holding on to something of sentiments, which would have caused Lot to still be around; of which it was Revealed that after Lot separated himself from Abraham, Abraham was then brought into A New Relationship with God, which could not have happened if Lot did not separate himself from Abraham. This was a sign of A New Level of Holiness for Abraham.

Genesis Chapter 13:14-18.

"AND THE LORD SAID UNTO ABRAM, AFTER THAT LOT WAS SEPARATED FROM HIM, LIFT UP NOW THINE EYES, AND LOOK FROM THE PLACE WHERE THOU ART NORTHWARD, AND SOUTHWARD, AND EASTWARD, AND WESTWARD: FOR ALL THE LAND WHICH THOU SEEST, TO THEE WILL I GIVE IT, AND TO THY SEED FOR EVER. AND I WILL MAKE THY SEED AS THE DUST OF THE EARTH: SO THAT IF A MAN CAN NUMBER THE DUST OF THE EARTH, THEN SHALL THY SEED ALSO BE NUMBERED. ARISE, WALK THROUGH THE LAND IN THE LENGTH OF IT AND IN THE BREADTH OF IT; FOR I WILL GIVE IT UNTO THEE. THEN ABRAM REMOVED HIS TENT, AND CAME AND DWELT IN THE PLAIN OF MAMRE, WHICH IS IN HEBRON, AND BUILT THERE AN ALTAR UNTO THE LORD".

There is also the example of Jesus Christ, when he was on trial before Pilot and all those who accused Him; Jesus Christ LET GO of His Authority to Demonstrate that He Was God in Flesh, to Allow mere men to judge The King of kings and The Lord of lord; He Humbled Himself through Beatings; Disgrace; Abuse, and even to Death. All this took place, and He Was Still God; He Let Go and did not Give Up. Giving Up Manifest Death without Hope; while Letting Go, even if it cost death will spring forth The Revelation of Spiritual Divine Blessing from The Almighty God.

LORD I PRAY IN THE NAME OF JESUS CHRIST, THAT YOU WILL EMPOWER THE MINDS OF THOSE WHO HAVE READ THIS MESSAGE; THAT THERE WILL BE DEVELOPED THE ANOINTING TO BELIEVE THAT THERE IS GREAT POWER TO THOSE WHO ARE YOUR SAINT WHO HAVE RECEIVED THE REVELATION TO LET GO, AND KNOW THAT LETTING GO DOES NOT MEAN THAT WE HAVE GIVEN UP. FATHER I KNOW THAT YOU LOVE YOUR PEOPLE; I PRAY THAT YOU WILL ALLOW US TO BE PATIENT WHEN IT IS NECESSARY, TO BE OBEDIENT TO YOUR WORD AT ALL TIMES; HELP US LORD TO ALWAYS BE SEEKING TO GAIN MORE AND MORE KNOWLEDGE IN YOU, GRANT US WISDOM DEAR FATHER, THIS I PRAY IN THE MIGHTY NAME OF JESUS CHRIST, AMEN.

I Hope that this Message has been an Inspiration to all those who have read, to let us be Born in The Understanding that it is God's Will if we are found in a position that demands for us to just Let Go, and it does not mean that we have Given Up. Unto The Matchless God, to Him Be Glory, Honour and all Praise, Jesus Christ The Lamb of God. From The Ministry of The Church of Jesus Christ Fellowship Savannah Cross Ltd. God's Blessing. Pastor Lerone Dinnall.

THE DIFFERENCE BETWEEN GIVING UP TO THAT OF LETTING GO.

The Giving That Brings Forth God's Release.

Message # 62   **Date Started February 7, 2017**
                                    Date Finalized February 12, 2017.

2 Corinthians Chapter 9:6-9.

"But this I say, he which soweth sparingly shall reap also sparingly; and he which soweth bountifully shall reap also bountifully. Every man according as he purposeth in his heart, so let him give; not grudgingly, or of necessity: for God Loveth a cheerful giver. And God Is Able to Make all grace abound toward you; that ye, always having all sufficiency in all things, may abound to every good work. As it is written, he hath dispersed aboard; he hath given to the poor: his righteousness remaineth forever".

St Luke Chapter 6:38.

"Give, and it shall be given unto you; good measure, pressed down, and shaken together, and running over,

SHALL MEN GIVE INTO YOUR BOSOM. FOR WITH THE SAME MEASURE THAT YE METE WITHAL IT SHALL BE MEASURED TO YOU AGAIN".

St Matthew Chapter 10:42.

"AND WHOSOEVER SHALL GIVE TO DRINK UNTO ONE OF THESE LITTLE ONES A CUP OF COLD WATER ONLY IN THE NAME OF A DISCIPLE, VERILY I SAY UNTO YOU, HE SHALL IN NO WISE LOSE HIS REWARD".

I Greet The All Powerful God, The God of All Ages and Times, The God of both The Spiritual and The Physical; in The Name of Jesus Christ I Give Honor. I Truly believe that this is A Topic that should have been explored a long time before now; but everything must be done according to God's Perfect Timing, when it is that God Has Given The Inspiration in Mind for hands to type.

It is currently being expressed by this Generation and time, that there is a great lack of Understanding of God's Word for individuals to know exactly what it is that The Heavenly Father Sees fit as an Accepted Offering. It has been observed that the main purpose of which many attempt to give, is definitely not the way and with the true intention of how The Lord Taught and Expressed for His People to show the Kindness of Giving.

There is a spirit of Confusion that is roaming the World, which seeks to Train and to Influence the Minds of God's People, to think of Giving in a way that if they must Give, it must be that they have Manipulated the process of giving, to make sure that whatsoever they have Given, must be given with the Study and Science of being able to receive back again some, if not all of what they have initially given.

Now in God's Eyes, this is the main reason of which it is currently being seen in the World, that there is absolutely no Running over of the Outpouring of God's Divine Blessings upon People, upon Towns, upon Communities, upon Countries. Because as it stands right now, the Generation which is now, is quickly sliding away, because of a lack of Knowledge of God's Word, which brings forth God's Direction for Mankind.

Have a look around, and you will even Identify for yourself, that whatever people are giving in today's Environment, is not being given with the intentions to receive a reward from God Above; but rather it is being given with the intentions of saying:

"WHAT WILL YOU, THE PERSON THAT IS RECEIVING BE ABLE TO GIVE ME IN RETURN".

Because it is now a custom that many will not give until they have the full assurance of knowing what they will be receiving in return. And what is currently taking place in the World is a system called A Round Robin and definitely not God's Divine Blessing. A Round Robin, meaning that, Today there will be all the Provisions needed for a person's business or promotions to make as much money that they can make within the time of their season to promote; then after that person's season has come to an end, then the first person's season of whom it was; it is now that person's time and others to give of all the support of that which they can give, to make sure that another person can promote their business; and this activity continues and continues to as much people that are in the group of promotions. This activity can be compared to that of a Partner Scheme; which is by man's promotion and not by God's Divine Order or Blessings.

The Giving that Brings Forth God's Release: What is this Giving? _____

_____.

We can start off by looking on the First Recorded Offering / Sacrifice that was Presented to God, which is to be found in The Book of Genesis Chapter 4. It is Reported that there were two Brothers, sons of Adam and of Eve, Namely Cain the first born and Abel is brother. The time came that these two Brothers Offered an Offering unto God, of which the Offering of Abel brought forth Respect to God, while the Offering of Cain God Did Not Respect.

We can have a look on the life of king Saul; his life as an Offering God Rejected, by not causing him nor his Generation to be Established, to be able to sit upon the Throne of Israel, to be a Representative of a king that God Choose. Then we can have a look at the life of king David as an Offering to God. The Lord Said to Samuel:

"FILL THINE HORN WITH OIL, AND GO, I WILL SEND THEE

TO JESSE THE BETHLEHEMITE: FOR I HAVE PROVIDED ME A KING AMONG HIS SONS". 1 Samuel Chapter 16:1.

It is Amazing to see and behold The Choice of God; in that God Chooses base on The Destiny of the choices that the Individual will be making, to therefore Manifest The Will of God Being Done; to bring forth Glory, Honour and Praise to The King of kings and The Lord of all lords. And it's even more amazing to know that when God Chooses someone; it doesn't automatically mean that this Individual is Perfect in the sense that, this Individual will never make mistakes that will Displease God; but God Who Knows the End from the very Beginning, would have already Seen that the Reason and the Purpose of which He Has Chosen this Individual is for the Fact, that this Individual would have chosen most of life's Cross Road, to walk in the path that will bring forth A Release from God that will Forgive even the Sins that this person have committed.

This was the Life of king David; David Sinned not once or twice, but many times; but his overall life as an Offering before God, showed that this was an Offering that God Could Respect to Accept, in order to Release an Anointing upon the Life of David that saw even Jesus Christ The Lamb of God coming out of the very Lineage of David without Sin. God had Promised David that He Will Establish His Throne Forever. And this is what The Lord Looks on:

David when he was confronted by Nathan the Prophet, immediately accepted that he was wrong, and had Sinned, he wrote in Psalms 51. Asking God to Create in him a Clean heart, and Renew a Right Spirit in him; he said Cast me not away from Thy Presence, and Take Not Thy Holy Spirit from me; and also established the Fact that A Broken spirit and A Contrite Heart, God Will Not Despise. By bringing forth this Revelation; David allowed Future Generations to realize the Secret of what it takes for God to Accept our Offerings, even if we are found in a Position that we have Sinned Against God. We will receive forgiveness with this action of Repentance, even though we have sinned Against God; the journey of our walk will become a little more difficult, because there is no sins that is committed by man that will not carry some effects of that sin. If it is found in us an Heart that is broken because of past Sins, and now craves and desires to be mended by The Father, in the sense that there is found within us a movement of Repentance; David revealed, that a heart like this will always Receive God's Attention to Forgive, then to Release an Anointing of Blessing upon His People.

Here is a Fact: Before God Can Release an Anointing or Favors; God Must First Forgive. If there is no Forgiveness, there can be no Releasing of God's Blessing; this is something for us to think about the next time we Pray!

Here is a wakeup call for us: God Really and Truly has A Desire of Needing to Bless His People, and to Provide all that His People have need of; but there is always Conditions Applied. Isaiah Chapter 59:1&2. All of God's Promises Says; "IF", meaning, if the Giving that is given by us being Children of God, is in an Acceptable format, then God Will have no Choice but to Respect that which was given, and then in return Release His Blessings upon that Individual that have Investigated and sought Knowledge to Have the Understanding of what to do, and how to do what is required of them to do, in order for their Offerings to be Respected by God.

We have to remember The Message that The Lord Gave us; which Title is The King's Wine. If we are not looking on our Offerings Being A Special Wine that God Drinks, then we will not be in a Position to give the Offerings that will result in God Releasing His Blessings. Everything that we do in life is considered to be an Offering before God. Every walk we make is an Offering; every speech we make is an Offering; every action we do is an Offering and most Important, Every thought of the Mind in the Spiritual Realm is an Offering, even though that which is thought of is not yet Manifested by the Heart; it was by this type of Offering, The Lord Knew what the Offering of Lucifer was, even before he started to Manifest that which his Mind had Conceived.

The Lord Has Revealed that His Eyes look throughout the lifetime of an Individual, to fully analyze what The Offering would be like in its Entirety; therefore, no one can put a label on any person, because no one but God Can Tell what will be The Quality of the Offering that such a person will Offer to God.

Many persons look on other people's Blessings and wonder why is it that they have received such a Blessing; and continuing to wonder, they forget to take a look at the Offering that is Presented before God, that Forced God's Hand to Release an Anointing to show forth that He Has Accepted that which was Given to Him.

It is God that Manifest; it is God that Appoint; it is God that Makes the Hills to Represent to Mankind that He Can Elevate any man to be as high as the Mountain, and it is God that Makes the Valleys to Prove to man that if they Refuse Knowledge, God Will Allow them to be as low as the Valleys, and that Valley will act as A Spiritual Prison for all those who have Rejected The Knowledge of The Most High GOD.

There will be many that seeks for A Greater Glory and A Greater Anointing in God, but we are still to Understand that Greater Levels depends deeply on the Individual that is ready to make the Sacrifice to give of A Greater Offering, that will be Accepted and Respected by GOD, thus Causing God to Release A Greater Blessing. What we can be confident about is the Fact that, when God Releases Favors upon His People; those Favors are not for a Season, but instead, those Favors Last for a Lifetime, and if God Is Really Pleased, those Favors continue towards our Generation and their Generation to come; and it was all because of the Accepted, Respected Offering that we have Given to God.

I know this Message will be of Benefit to God's People, I only pray that you may keep this Ministry in your Prayers, and also remember My Family, May God Continue to Bless, Keep and Prosper your going out and your coming in, from this time forth and forevermore. To God Be All The Glory from Everlasting to Eternity. Pastor Lerone Dinnall.

THE GIVING THAT BRINGS FORTH GOD'S RELEASE. GOD IS WAITING ON OUR CLEAN SACRIFICE IN ORDER TO RELEASE HIS DIVINE BLESSINGS.

WHY DOES GOD'S BEST, APPEARS TO BE MY WORSE?

Message # 37

Date Started September 12, 2016
Date Finalized September 16, 2016.

To GOD BE THE Glory, Great Things He Had Done. Happy and Honored to be writing for God's People Another Inspired Message from God The Father, and Our True Saviour Jesus Christ. I wonder at times, where these Messages come from, but then I remember that they are Inspired by God, to speak to a situation that A Child of God may be Experiencing.

The first Question to ask Is: Have you ever felt like this, concerning what the Topic is asking us to look into? _____ _____.

If it is that God Has A Good Plan for your life, trust me, you're going to feel exactly what the Topic is Expressing.

WHAT IS GOOD?

Good is explain as being Morally Excellent; Virtuous; Righteous; Satisfactory in Quality; High Quality; Excellent.

By what is explained of the word good, you would have thought that it is something to look forward to, of which it is, but we will soon learn that there is a journey.

There is a saying that goes like this:

"YOU SEE THE GLORY, BUT YOU DON'T KNOW THE STORY"

There is another that says:

"IF YOU NEED GOOD, YOUR NOSE HAS TO RUN"

And to think about it, where just talking about the word Good, we have not even started to consider of God's Best. Although it can be said that anything that God Has Given to His People, must be considered to be Good, which should result in God's Best. I am reminded of A Scripture in The Bible that Said:

"FOR I KNOW THE THOUGHTS THAT I THINK TOWARDS YOU, SAITH THE LORD, THOUGHTS OF PEACE, AND NOT EVIL, TO GIVE YOU AN EXPECTED END". Jeremiah Chapter 29:11.

There are many times I ask myself this Question: What if God Never Desired Good for His People, what would happen? _____ _____.

Answer: Complete destruction of the Human race.

The Lord Said, His Thoughts for us are peaceful; but then, we wonder, with all that I'm going through, can this really result in being of benefit to me? _____ _____.

A Professor spoke one day in a seminar, and he was speaking of a path and direction to success, and he went on to say that Success is spelt one way, and that's HARD WORK. If you're not prepared to do hard work, then you cannot obtain Success. I can use that same sentence and say, if you're not prepared to work the hardest you've ever worked, then you won't receive Good, which is God's Best.

Let me bring to your remembrance; Abraham, when he was told to Separate from his people and country, unto a place that God Would Reveal to him for A Blessing; Abraham after moving by faith, discovered that God's Blessing brought along with moving these words called Struggles, Testing, A Stronger belief to overcome, Famine and also Fear of what the enemy would do to him and his wife. It brought forth Doubt concerning the promised child, it brought forth Patience of waiting for twenty-five years to see the promise of a son being fulfilled, only to hear The Lord Asked you to get back in a position that you're going to lose that son that He Gave to you.

I find myself many of the time, when I'm experiencing one of these challenges, asking God, Why me, Why me; The Voice of God Came Back to me and Said:

1. WHY NOT YOU?
2. ARE YOU NOT SET FOR GREAT BLESSING!
3. WAS IT NOT SPOKEN OVER YOUR LIFE, THAT YOU SHOULD BE THE HEAD, AND NOT THE TALE!
4. ARE YOU NOT SET TO BE A ROYAL PRIESTHOOD, HOLY NATION, AND A PECULIAR PEOPLE!
5. HOW DO YOU THINK, YOU'RE GOING TO BE, WHAT I NEED YOU TO BE WITHOUT THE FIRE;
6. I HAVE TO BURN OFF EVERYTHING THAT IS ON YOU AND IN YOU, THAT DON'T RESEMBLE THE INHERITANCE OF MY BLESSING.
7. WAIT ON MY TIMING.

My only response to that was:

"NOT MY WILL LORD, BUT YOUR WILL BE DONE IN MY LIFE".

We can remember clearly, that John the Baptist made mention that Jesus Christ must increase but I John must decrease. This passage of Scripture is expressed by many of us to acknowledge that, the desire and the will of the man must be crucified, put to death, in order for The Revelation and Will of God to take complete control over our lives. John continued by saying:

"HE THAT COMETH FROM ABOVE IS ABOVE ALL; HE THAT IS OF THE EARTH IS EARTHLY, AND SPEAKETH OF THE EARTH; HE

THAT COMETH FROM HEAVEN IS ABOVE ALL". St John Chapter 3:30&31.

I made mention of this passage of Scripture because, everything that must resemble The Best of God in our life, must be Reflecting that which comes from Heaven; and coming from Heaven means that it is not Natural, or of this World; but something special that seeks to Release an Anointing that comes from God The Father; which will Bring forth The Revelation of something Supernatural in our lives, that not only comes for a Season, but to make a complete difference in our lives that will last for Eternity.

Let us learn something about God; whenever He Gives A Command for Blessing upon an individual, that Blessing is destined to fulfill A Lifetime of Deliverance, and no one can stop it. Romans Chapter 8:31.

"WHAT SHALL WE THEN SAY TO THESE THING? IF GOD BE FOR US, WHO CAN BE AGAINST US?" _____

_____.

Let's take a look at the life of Joseph; it must have felt good for Joseph receiving those Visions from God, Revealing to him what was his True Destiny. Joseph felt so good that he could not keep the joy of what he saw, or being a youth, The Bible Said that he was seventeen (17) years old; maybe it was that he could not yet understand what the dreams meant, therefore, decided to reveal what he dreamt, to discover the Revelations of his dreams.

I have listen to many people making mention to this Story, by saying that Joseph was being Boastful; but I'm not in agreement with those thoughts. Upon reading The Bible carefully, I discover that Joseph never began to be the interpreter of dreams until he was in prison; there is no other evidence in The Bible to suggest that Joseph when he was young, understood what he dreamt. This I strongly believe, because Gifts from God Comes in Portions, and at Smaller Levels before it advances to Bigger Levels.

Samuel the Prophet was such a person, when he was a child he could not discern The Voice of God; it took Eli, a prophet that was more advance to explain to Samuel that The Voice he was hearing was indeed The Voice of God and not man, and told him exactly how to Answer The Lord when He Calls the next time.

Also I discover that when God Has A Destiny for a person, that Destiny Is Revealed in portions, and only what is necessary for that person to receive at that point in their life will that person be able to receive from God.

PROOF: God Revealed to Joseph a dream or dreams in parable, that he may not have understood what it meant; do you realize that God Did Not Revealed to Joseph THE HARDSHIP that he was to face being just seventeen years old; because if it is that God Showed him what was going to happen to him, he would have stayed far away from his brothers, but in innocence, he went and obeyed the command of his father to look and to be of some aid to his brothers, not knowing the evil intent that was plan to destroy his life. To fulfill the words that says, that which is meant for evil, God Destined from evil, His Best for my Life.

It is amazing to see that in every Victory that God Has for His People, it has to come through Darkness. The Bible Reveals to us that God Called Light from Darkness; therefore, we should not be surprise that our Victory coming from God must follow a similar experience, that the life of God's People Have to go through this pathway of Darkness in order to find Light. Was not our Salvation brought forth through the suffering and death of Jesus Christ Our Lord and Saviour? _____

_____.

My advice to those of us that has an expectation to Receive of God's Best; try to prepare yourself for the Struggles you have to face, in order to reap the rewards of The Blessing of God's Best. This story of the Rich Young Ruler has to be in this Message; this young man, according to The Bible, was living up to the Standard of what The Laws of God Required him to live, but there was still a But; he came to Jesus Christ Desiring something that could not be achieve by only following the Rules by the Letter; but discovered that Jesus Christ Ask him to do something that will prove, that he wasn't just interested in following The Laws of God by the action he did daily;

but to produce a Final Test, just like what God did to Abraham to prove that his desire and love far exceed the love of any material thing that can be possessed on earth.

Through these words of mine, I'm making reference to the fact that I believe that the Rich Young Ruler was just being given a Final Test from God, to manifest if his love and desire was truly to Inherit Eternal Life. This Test, the Young Ruler, that for all his years did his best to follow the Laws of God, he Failed; proving that his love was more for that which he possessed in this life. The Lord Said, How hard it is for those that have riches, to enter The Kingdom of Heaven; but also made us realized that, what is impossible for man, is possible for God. I believe that God Was Able to Change that Rich Young Ruler's life; it wasn't listed in The Bible, but The Lord Is Able to Make Possible, that which is Impossible.

I know that the Standard for God is complete surrender; but is God Not Patient in Action, not to take in consideration that this young man was, by his own testimony, and by The Revelation of what God Discern, was doing what He Commanded Israel to Do in The Ten Commandments. I believe that this Young Ruler was able to receive Salvation, if not by the preaching of Jesus Christ, then by the preaching of The Ministry He left behind.

The Lord Jesus Christ Revealed in The Scriptures that, the Young Ruler by going away sorrowful, missed out on receiving TREASURES IN HEAVEN; not that he would never Inherit Heaven. Because if you're on the pathway that leads to Heaven, the only thing that can prevent you from entering, is to come directly off the path way. The Bible Said nothing else about the Rich Young Ruler, therefore, there is no guideline to say that he stop living according to The Requirements of the Law; or even to let us know that he got A Vision from God, that Encouraged him to do what was asked of him to Do.

Let me bring our Minds to remembrance of what The Words of God Reveals, The Bible Said that after the day of Pentecost, many of the disciples sold lands and possessions and laid the income from those things that was sold at the Apostles feet. Could not one of those persons be The Rich Young Ruler? _____

_____.

Speaking personally over my life, I would not want to know that I have been trying my best to do everything in my power to live a God fearing life, only to hear that God Will Not Do All in His Power to ensure that I receive the prize for that which am working for. I don't care by what means God Takes Action to Help me to make it through that Gate of Heaven, just Do It Lord.

Let us consider those who are not doing what God Asked them to Do; they can never Enter Heaven, no problem; then compare it to a man, that is only short by one mark; Is God Not Going to Help? _____

_____.

I believe He Will; I believe God Did Help that Rich Young Ruler to understand the True Value of Heaven; that it can never be in comparison to anything on Earth. Therefore, if it is that we need help to surrender all to Jesus Christ; it is my belief that God Will Help.

Stand for a minute in the life of The Rich Young Ruler; this must have been the hardest thing anyone could have ever asked him to do; it is hard, but it is also necessary. Receiving of God's Best, appears to be my worst; but it only APPEARS. The worse of our life, will only last for a season; then after the season is accomplished, what else is there to receive but The Joy that God Has In Store for us. Things that will assist us to go through our worst, is Prayer Continually, Effective Fasting, this is The Spiritual Food for The Spirit that is in us, otherwise known as The Word of God, The Holy Ghost, The Clean Spirit from The Father.

Let us Stay far away from people, who just don't understand the process that God Is Allowing us to Go Through, they are known as THE FAITHLESS; they will only make us feel worse than what we are going through, keep friends that can encourage you, and Pray for you. In your Prayers make sure you tell God Everything, let Him be your number one Comforter, Listen only to Positive Preachers and Teachers, because our Soul is A Soil, we have to be very careful of the type of SEEDS we allow to be planted in our Soils; some seeds will seek to destroy our foundation, and let us believe that God Is Not Working Things Out for Our Good.

Let us be Positive in everything we do, it will shine right back on our lives. Don't allow our experience to influence the way we treat others, treat everyone the way we would need them to treat us; just remember, this life that were living in, its only ONE BIG TEST, go through it with patience, look on it as a challenge the devil made before God concerning our life; he's just waiting to see us make a mistake, just to do something out of The Characteristic of God, so that he can boast before God and say, I TOLD YOU SO.

Don't allow that little fella to have the last laugh over our lives. I have been through challenges in my life that The Lord's Response to me was:

"IT IS JUST A TEST".

Remember that what we are going through is just A Test, how long will it last, only God Knows.

People of God, while going through your TEST remember that no Test last forever; it must end one day. Make sure when it ends, you have OVERCOME, and not failed what was only A Test. There is one important thing to remember: It is God that Sets The Test, and therefore, He Has Already Put in you the Necessary Ingredient for you to pass that Test. Always remember, what doesn't kill you, only make you stronger; you're not built to break.

1 Corinthians Chapter 10:13. Says:

"THERE HATH NO TEMPTATION TAKEN YOU BUT SUCH AS IS COMMON TO MAN: BUT GOD IS FAITHFUL, WHO WILL NOT SUFFER YOU TO BE TEMPTED ABOVE THAT YE ARE ABLE; BUT WILL WITH THE TEMPTATION ALSO MAKE A WAY TO ESCAPE, THAT YE MAY BE ABLE TO BEAR IT".

There comes a time in our Test, that we will realize that it's better for us to remain standing UPRIGHT, rather than to find ourselves starting to Bend / Compromise. It is The Spirit of God in us that is going to allow us to have The Revelation to know that God Has Better for us; even if our Test cause us to die the physical death.

Did not The Lord Said:

"FEAR NOT THEM WHICH KILL THE BODY, BUT ARE NOT ABLE TO KILL THE SOUL; BUT RATHER FEAR HIM WHICH IS ABLE TO DESTROY BOTH SOUL AND BODY IN HELL". St Matthew Chapter 10:29.

I am reminded of the Story in The Book of Daniel Chapter 6. How that Daniel, a man who was Greatly Beloved by God, knew of a Decree that was signed, concerning offering Prayer to his God; because Daniel knew that Praying to God was a must, he did not care about what the king had signed. The Bible Says that Daniel knew that the Decree was sign, he went into his house; his windows being opened, he kneeled and prayed three times for the day, as he was accustom to do, and gave thanks. Can you just imagine, the decree is signed that I must die if I Pray; and on my knees I find my lips speaking in a language that it is offering thanks to God, instead of asking God to Send me some way of Deliverance. WOW! Now we can identify that levels in Prayers does exits, levels in Relationship with God is very important.

Daniel went through the experience of the lion's den, but the lion could not harm a hair on his head, because God Did Not Allow them; no wonder Daniel in his Prayers was Giving God Thanks. He must have received A Vision of what the outcome would be like, therefore, the only thing left to do was to say Thank You Lord for The TEST.

If there is one thing that these Stories in The Bible Teaches, is that those who esteem themselves to be Servants of The Living God, cannot find themselves in a position that they are afraid to die for The Standard of what God Allows them to Believe in. The Bible is for our Example to Teach us that even if our Test / Worse, results in us leaving this life, then we've got to find ourselves in a position that were so much FULL OF THE HOLY GHOST, that it doesn't matter anymore what man want to do to our lives; because we are Confident that God Has Prepared for us A Place that is free from All Test.

Why Does God's Best, appears to be my worse; after considering all the evidence of this Message, we can now say, as long as it is The Will of God, that I suffer many things in this life; I open my heart fully to receive the challenges of this life, which will cement My Soul in the life that Is ETERNAL.

It's never the beginning of a man; it's always the ending, that's what is Important for us to keep our eyes on. Make sure we finish THE TEST. Those that suffer with Christ, shall Reign with Christ. There is no Testimony, until we have passed The Test.

May God Bless, Keep, Encourage, Sustain, Feed you with His Word that you may be Full. From Your Friend, Your Minister and Pastor Lerone Dinnall.

WHY DOES GOD'S BEST APPEARS TO BE MY WORSE!

A SUCCESSFUL MINISTRY

SEEKING TO KNOW THE THREE W'S, THE WHAT, THE WHY AND THE WHEN.

Message # 65

Date Started February 25, 2017.
Date Finalized March 5, 2017.

WHAT IS THE FOUNDATION OF A SUCCESSFUL MINISTRY?

ROMANS CHAPTER 8:28-31.

"AND WE KNOW THAT ALL THINGS WORK TOGETHER FOR GOOD TO THEM THAT LOVE GOD, TO THEM WHO ARE THE CALLED ACCORDING TO HIS PURPOSE. FOR WHOM HE DID FOREKNOW, HE ALSO DID PREDESTINATE TO BE CONFORMED TO THE IMAGE OF HIS SON, THAT HE MIGHT BE THE FIRSTBORN AMONG MANY BRETHREN. MOREOVER WHOM HE DID PREDESTINATE,

THEM HE ALSO CALLED: AND WHOM HE CALLED, THEM HE ALSO JUSTIFIED: AND WHOM HE JUSTIFIED, THEM HE ALSO GLORIFIED. WHAT SHALL WE THEN SAY TO THESE THINGS? IF GOD BE FOR US, WHO CAN BE AGAINST US"?

St Matthew Chapter 16:13-19.

"WHEN JESUS CAME INTO THE COASTS OF CAESAREA PHILIPPI, HE ASKED HIS DISCIPLES, SAYING, WHOM DO MEN SAY THAT I THE SON OF MAN AM? AND THEY SAID, SOME SAY THAT THOU ART JOHN THE BAPTIST: SOME, ELIAS; AND OTHERS, JEREMIAS, OR ONE OF THE PROPHETS. HE SAITH UNTO THEM, BUT WHOM SAY YE THAT I AM? AND SIMON PETER ANSWERED AND SAID, THOU ART THE CHRIST, THE SON OF THE LIVING GOD. AND JESUS ANSWERED AND SAID UNTO HIM, BLESSED ART THOU, SIMON BARJONA: FOR FLESH AND BLOOD HATH NOT REVEALED IT UNTO THEE, BUT MY FATHER WHICH IS IN HEAVEN. AND I SAY ALSO UNTO THEE, THAT THOU ART PETER, AND UPON THIS ROCK I WILL BUILD MY CHURCH; AND THE GATES OF HELL SHALL NOT PREVAIL AGAINST IT. AND I WILL GIVE UNTO THEE THE KEYS OF THE KINGDOM OF HEAVEN: AND WHATSOEVER THOU SHALT BIND ON EARTH SHALL BE BOUND IN HEAVEN; AND WHATSOEVER THOU SHALT LOOSE ON EARTH SHALL BE LOOSED IN HEAVEN".

NOTE: This promise was upon the confession and the acknowledgement that Jesus Christ Is indeed The Rock, The True Manifestation of The Word of God; therefore, The Lord Jesus Christ was allowing Peter and also those of us who read with understanding to know that whatever is being Built on The Revelation of The Word of God, which is Jesus Christ, will suffer many challenges, but the end product of all those who remain upon this Revelation to walk in this belief, will realize The True Revelation of The Authority of God upon their lives. An Authority that speaks towards everything that we Declare on Earth will be Decreed in Heaven; and everything we Declare to be done in The Spiritual, will be and must be Manifested in the Physical, because Jesus Christ Is The Complete Fulfillment of The God Head.

Exodus Chapter 3:14-15.

"AND GOD SAID UNTO MOSES, I AM THAT I AM: AND HE SAID, THUS SHALT THOU SAY UNTO THE CHILDREN OF ISRAEL, I AM HATH SENT ME UNTO YOU. AND GOD SAID MOREOVER UNTO MOSES, THUS SHALT THOU SAY UNTO THE CHILDREN OF ISRAEL, THE GOD OF YOUR FATHERS, THE GOD OF ABRAHAM, THE GOD OF ISAAC, AND THE GOD OF JACOB, HATH SENT ME UNTO YOU: THIS IS MY NAME FOREVER, AND THIS IS MY MEMORIAL UNTO ALL GENERATIONS".

NOTE: To know that God Fills all things should be of Great comfort for all who desires a Relationship with God; Moses at that time was very timid to move towards God's Instructions, but found out that once he began to move in The Belief and The Revelation that it is God The I AM, that Fills everything, and Allow for everything to come into Existence, then the man Moses was no longer timid or afraid to open his mouth to speak, but found out that he now Develop A Boldness of Character to Resemble The Character of THE I AM THAT I AM.

Acts Chapter 2:38.

"THEN PETER SAID UNTO THEM, REPENT, AND BE BAPTIZED EVERY ONE OF YOU IN THE NAME OF JESUS CHRIST FOR THE REMISSION OF SINS, AND YE SHALL RECEIVE THE GIFT OF THE HOLY GHOST".

NOTE: A Successful Ministry will never be built with members that have not yet Repented of their Sins, but before a member comes to the acknowledgement that Repentance is a must, that member must first be Born in the belief that Jesus Christ Is God, and only through Him is The Access Door for The Salvation of mankind; then after the belief is born and Repentance has been walked, then and only then will Baptism be a fulfillment to Bury the Old man, thus causing The New man to have all the ingrediente to be now able to fulfill all The Purpose and The Requirements of The Almighty God; therefore now allowing for the Access of this Individual to now be able to Receive The Infilling of The Holy Ghost, The True Conscience of The Almighty God.

Acts Chapter 4:8-13.

"THEN PETER, FILLED WITH THE HOLY GHOST, SAID UNTO THEM, YE RULERS OF THE PEOPLE, AND ELDERS OF ISRAEL, IF WE THIS DAY BE EXAMINED OF THE GOOD DEED DONE TO THE IMPOTENT MAN, BY WHAT MEANS HE IS MADE WHOLE; BE IT KNOWN UNTO YOU ALL, AND TO ALL THE PEOPLE OF ISRAEL, THAT BY THE NAME OF JESUS CHRIST OF NAZARETH, WHOM YE CRUCIFIED, WHOM GOD RAISED FROM THE DEAD, EVEN BY HIM DOTH THIS MAN STAND HERE BEFORE YOU WHOLE. THIS IS THE STONE WHICH WAS SET AT NOUGHT OF YOU BUILDERS, WHICH IS BECOME THE HEAD OF THE CORNER. NEITHER IS THERE SALVATION IN ANY OTHER: FOR THERE IS NONE OTHER NAME UNDER HEAVEN GIVEN AMONG MEN, WHEREBY WE MUST BE SAVED. NOW WHEN THEY SAW THE BOLDNESS OF PETER AND JOHN, AND PERCEIVED THAT THEY WERE UNLEARNED AND IGNORANT MEN, THEY TOOK KNOWLEDGE OF THEM, THAT THEY HAD BEEN WITH JESUS".

NOTE: The Revelation of Jesus Christ is The Foundation in every Successful Ministry; without God at The Head of Everything that is being Taught and Preached, then that Ministry is being Built on Sand and not on THE ROCK. Which means that whatever is being done for Ministry without the evidence of Jesus Christ being The Foundation, it will not stand, and will only go on for a season and for a time, until the Storms arise, then it will be Blown away, as leaf to the Wind.

St John Chapter 10:7-10.

"THEN SAID JESUS UNTO THEM AGAIN, VERILY, VERILY, I SAY UNTO YOU, I AM THE DOOR OF THE SHEEP. ALL THAT EVER CAME BEFORE ME ARE THIEVES AND ROBBERS: BUT THE SHEEP DID NOT HEAR THEM. I AM THE DOOR: BY ME IF ANY MAN ENTER IN, HE SHALL BE SAVED, AND SHALL GO IN AND OUT, AND FIND PASTURE. THE THIEF COMETH NOT, BUT FOR TO STEAL, AND TO KILL, AND TO DESTROY: I AM COME THAT THEY MIGHT HAVE LIFE, AND THAT THEY MIGHT HAVE IT MORE ABUNDANTLY".

NOTE: Knowing that Jesus Christ Is The Door is one thing, being able to walk in The Character of The Requirements of The Access Door is a complete different story. How can a person say that they believe that Jesus Christ Is God, and instead are not desirous to do and to walk in every Will and Commands that Jesus Christ Asked us to walk in. If we say we Believe in Him and don't do what He Says; that is spelt Confusion and Hypocrisy.

Having The Foundation of knowing Who and What God Stands for is extremely Important, because God and God Alone Is The Only True and Sure Foundation; therefore, being in Ministry we will Identify Who Exactly is The Corner Stone of what we are Building upon, which is GOD, Manifested In Jesus Christ.

WHY IS SEPARATION / HOLINESS ONE OF THE MOST IMPORTANT INGREDIENCE IN THE FOUNDATION OF A SUCCESSFUL MINISTRY?

Genesis Chapter 12:1-3.

"NOW THE LORD HAD SAID UNTO ABRAM, GET THEE OUT OF THY COUNTRY, AND FROM THY KINDRED, AND FROM THY FATHER'S HOUSE, UNTO A LAND THAT I WILL SHEW THEE: AND I WILL MAKE OF THEE A GREAT NATION, AND I WILL BLESS THEE, AND MAKE THY NAME GREAT; AND THOU SHALT BE A BLESSING: AND I WILL BLESS THEM THAT BLESS THEE, AND CURSE HIM THAT CURSETH THEE: AND IN THEE SHALL ALL FAMILIES OF THE EARTH BE BLESSED".

NOTE: Every person wants and need to step into THE WILL OF GOD, but finds that we have not yet come into The Revelation to know that for us to receive of GOD'S WILL / GOD'S DIVINE BLESSINGS, there must be A Separation, which Is HOLINESS.

Holiness begins with believing in God and therefore turning to make an Earnest desire to walk in the paths of Righteousness.

St Luke Chapter 24:49.

"AND BEHOLD I SEND THE PROMISE OF MY FATHER UPON

YOU: BUT TARRY YE IN THE CITY OF JERUSALEM, UNTIL YE BE ENDUED WITH POWER FROM ON HIGH".

Acts Chapter 1:4-5.

"AND BEING ASSEMBLED TOGETHER WITH THEM, COMMANDED THEM THAT THEY SHOULD NOT DEPART FROM JERUSALEM, BUT WAIT FOR THE PROMISE OF THE FATHER, WHICH, SAITH HE, YE HAVE HEARD OF ME. FOR JOHN TRULY BAPTIZED WITH WATER; BUT YE SHALL BE BAPTIZED WITH THE HOLY GHOST NOT MANY DAYS HENCE".

NOTE: For the Disciples to Receive The Holy Ghost, they had to be Separated from everything and anything that will cause them not to Receive of The True Spirit of God.

St Luke Chapter 8:49-56.

"WHILE HE YET SPAKE, THERE COMETH ONE FROM THE RULER OF THE SYNAGOGUE'S HOUSE, SAYING TO HIM, THY DAUGHTER IS DEAD; TROUBLE NOT THE MASTER. BUT WHEN JESUS HEARD IT, HE ANSWERED HIM, SAYING, FEAR NOT: BELIEVE ONLY, AND SHE SHALL BE MADE WHOLE. AND WHEN HE CAME INTO THE HOUSE, HE SUFFERED NO MAN TO GO IN, SAVE PETER, AND JAMES, AND JOHN, AND THE FATHER AND THE MOTHER OF THE MAIDEN. AND ALL WEPT, AND BEWAILED HER: BUT HE SAID, WEEP NOT; SHE IS NOT DEAD, BUT SLEEPETH. AND THEY LAUGHED HIM TO SCORN, KNOWING THAT SHE WAS DEAD. AND HE PUT THEM ALL OUT, AND TOOK HER BY THE HAND, AND CALLED, SAYING, MAID, ARISE. AND HER SPIRIT CAME AGAIN, AND SHE AROSE STRAIGHTWAY: AND HE COMMANDED TO GIVE HER MEAT. AND HER PARENTS WERE ASTONISHED: BUT HE CHARGED THEM THAT THEY SHOULD TELL NO MAN WHAT WAS DONE".

NOTE: Great works and Miracles cannot be accomplished around Doubters and Unbelievers of The Ministry of Jesus Christ. Therefore, there will be times when we need for God to Work, we have got to select members that are True Believers to come into Prayer, to then allow for The Release of God's Favor. Where two or three are gathered, there am I in the midst, to Hear their Cry and to Answer their Request.

St Matthew Chapter 9:14-17.

"THEN CAME TO HIM THE DISCIPLES OF JOHN, SAYING, WHY DO WE AND THE PHARISEES FAST OFT, BUT THY DISCIPLES FAST NOT? AND JESUS SAID UNTO THEM, CAN THE CHILDREN OF THE BRIDECHAMBER MOURN, AS LONG AS THE BRIDEGROOM IS WITH THEM? BUT THE DAYS WILL COME, WHEN THE BRIDEGROOM SHALL BE TAKEN FROM THEM, AND THEN SHALL THEY FAST. NO MAN PUTTETH A PIECE OF NEW CLOTH UNTO AN OLD GARMENT, FOR THAT WHICH IS PUT IN TO FILL IT UP TAKETH FROM THE GARMENT, AND THE RENT IS MADE WORSE. NEITHER DO MEN PUT NEW WINE INTO OLD BOTTLES: ELSE THE BOTTLES BREAK, AND THE WINE RUNNETH OUT, AND THE BOTTLES PERISH: BUT THEY PUT NEW WINE INTO NEW BOTTLES, AND BOTH ARE PRESERVED".

NOTE: It must be understood that for A Ministry to be Successful, that Ministry needs A Foundation that is laid on Spirit and Truth, if this is not realized then whatever is being built, is only being built on Unrighteousness, which cannot stand and will never stand.

St John Chapter 3:3-5.

"JESUS ANSWERED AND SAID UNTO HIM, VERILY, verily, I SAY UNTO THEE, EXCEPT A MAN BE BORN AGAIN, HE CANNOT SEE THE KINGDOM OF GOD. NICODEMUS SAITH UNTO HIM, HOW CAN A MAN BE BORN WHEN HE IS OLD? CAN HE ENTER THE SECOND TIME INTO HIS MOTHER'S WOMB, AND BE BORN? JESUS ANSWERED, VERILY, verily, I SAY UNTO THEE, EXCEPT A MAN BE BORN OF WATER AND OF THE SPIRIT, HE CANNOT ENTER INTO THE KINGDOM OF GOD".

NOTE: It is important to come to the knowledge of the Facts: A Successful Ministry Cannot Be Built with people that are not BORN AGAIN. This is a Big waste of Time and Energy and Resources. It is better to start The Foundation of Ministry with the Young Repented Soul, than to waste time with those that are stuck in their own ways of doing what they believe is to be done.

I remembered being on The Hill that God Placed me, and desiring to see Things and Project of The Church Move Forward; The Lord Response to me Was:

"CAN RIGHTEOUSNESS BE BUILT ON UNRIGHTEOUSNESS"?

After hearing those words, I then realize that Ministry Is A Patient Work; it takes time for members of The Church to Become Righteous in order for God to Release the Permission of Growth. Do only what is necessary for Ministry, and Leave the rest for God to Give the Increase. The Increase Comes from God, and only God Alone Can Make and Allow Saints to Become Righteous / Lively Stones to Build up The Spiritual House.

WHEN IS MINISTRY EFFECTIVE?

Ministry Becomes Effective, when we are not only Called, but have received The Spirit of Obedience towards The Direction of God's Will by His Wisdom. Remember that Ministry Is Completely God's Will and not the Will of man. One of the Most Important thing in Ministry is to know when to Move and to know how to Act and What and Who to use, in whatever Positions they are to be used in.

Proverbs Chapter 3:5-6.

"TRUST IN THE LORD WITH ALL THINE HEART; AND LEAN NOT UNTO THINE OWN UNDERSTANDING. IN ALL THY WAYS ACKNOWLEDGE HIM, AND HE WILL DIRECT THY PATHS".

2 Samuels Chapter 5:17-19 & Verse 22-25.

"BUT WHEN THE PHILISTINES HEARD THAT THEY HAD ANOINTED DAVID KING OVER ISRAEL, ALL THE PHILISTINES CAME UP TO SEEK DAVID; AND DAVID HEARD OF IT, AND WENT DOWN TO THE HOLD. THE PHILISTINES ALSO CAME AND SPREAD THEMSELVES IN THE VALLEY OF REPHAIM. AND DAVID INQUIRED OF THE LORD, SAYING, SHALL I GO UP TO THE PHILISTINES? WILT THOU DELIVER THEM INTO MINE HAND? AND THE LORD SAID UNTO DAVID, GO UP: FOR I WILL DOUBTLESS DELIVER THE PHILISTINES INTO THINE HAND".

"AND THE PHILISTINES CAME UP YET AGAIN, AND SPREAD THEMSELVES IN THE VALLEY OF REPHAIM. AND WHEN DAVID INQUIRED OF THE LORD, HE SAID, THOU SHALT NOT GO UP; BUT FETCH A COMPASS BEHIND THEM, AND COME UPON THEM OVER AGAINST THE MULBERRY TREES. AND LET IT BE, WHEN THOU HEAREST THE SOUND OF A GOING IN THE TOPS OF THE MULBERRY TREES, THAT THEN THOU SHALT BESTIR THYSELF: FOR THEN SHALL THE LORD GO OUT BEFORE THEE, TO SMITE THE HOST OF THE PHILISTINES. AND DAVID DID SO, AS THE LORD HAD COMMANDED HIM; AND SMOTE THE PHILISTINES FROM GEBA UNTIL THOU COME TO GAZER".

Judges Chapter 7:4-7.

"AND THE LORD SAID UNTO GIDEON, THE PEOPLE ARE YET TOO MANY; BRING THEM DOWN UNTO THE WATER, AND I WILL TRY THEM FOR THEE THERE: AND IT SHALL BE, THAT WHOM I SAY UNTO THEE, THIS SHALL GO WITH THEE, THE SAME SHALL GO WITH THEE, AND OF WHOSOEVER I SAY UNTO THEE, THIS SHALL NOT GO WITH THEE, THE SAME SHALL NOT GO. SO HE BROUGHT DOWN THE PEOPLE UNTO THE WATER: AND THE LORD SAID UNTO GIDEON, EVERY ONE THAT LAPPETH OF THE WATER WITH HIS TONGUE, AS A DOG LAPPET, HIM SHALT THOU SET BY HIMSELF; LIKEWISE EVERYONE THAT BOWETH DOWN UPON HIS KNEES TO DRINK. AND THE NUMBER OF THEM THAT LAPPED, PUTTING THEIR HAND TO THEIR MOUTH, WERE THREE HUNDRED MEN: BUT ALL THE REST OF THE PEOPLE BOWED DOWN UPON HIS KNEES TO DRINK WATER. AND THE LORD SAID UNTO GIDEON, BY THE THREE HUNDRED MEN THAT LAPPED WILL I SAVE YOU, AND DELIVER THE MIDIANITES INTO THINE HAND: AND LET ALL THE OTHER PEOPLE GO EVERY MAN UNTO HIS PLACE".

NOTE: It was 0.9375 of the percentage of what Gideon originally had that God Used to Deliver him from the Midianites. The original number was 32,000 men, and God Used less than 1% of those men to bring forth Victory. God's Strength Is Not in Quantity, but in Quality of those who Reflect His Spirit. It's not who commended himself is Approved, but whom The Lord Commended. Ministry is not for those who will say yes I will go, but it's for those who God Deems Worthy of the Journey. Ministry is Called and Placed for a specific Time and Purpose; to Attract not all, but a specific type of People Which God Requires as Being His Tenth. Therefore, let us not be confused; not all people that is on the earth will be Saved, or even take heed to their ways, to be in The Mind of God for a Consideration of being Called for Salvation.

God Knoweth The End from the very Beginning, and He Knows those who are willing to Surrender to The Call of Salvation; therefore, while it is that it is God that Builds A Successful Ministry, it must also be placed in our Minds that, those who are to be Saved, will become Saved. We are mere Tools in The Hands of God, set in a Position to do A Worthy Job.

When I was first Commissioned to Build an Altar for The Lord; The Lord Told me to Stand upon Holiness because it will be my strength, and also to make me know that not everyone is going to get Saved; therefore, I should not be surprised with just a little amount of people that are willing to follow God's Command. To understand Ministry a little more, I would advise that each person desiring to endure Ministry to read 2 Timothy Chapter 4:1-5 continually.

"I CHARGE THEE THEREFORE BEFORE GOD, AND THE LORD JESUS CHRIST, WHO SHALL JUDGE THE QUICK AND THE DEAD AT HIS APPEARING AND HIS KINGDOM; PREACH THE WORD; BE INSTANT IN SEASON, OUT OF SEASON; REPROVE, REBUKE, EXHORT WITH ALL LONGSUFFERING AND DOCTRINE. FOR THE TIME WILL COME WHEN THEY WILL NOT ENDURE SOUND DOCTRINE; BUT AFTER THEIR OWN LUSTS SHALL THEY HEAP TO THEMSELVES TEACHERS, HAVING ITCHING EARS; AND THEY SHALL TURN AWAY THEIR EARS FROM THE TRUTH, AND SHALL BE TURNED UNTO FABLES. BUT WATCH THOU IN ALL THINGS, ENDURE AFFLICTIONS, DO THE WORK OF AN EVANGELIST, MAKE FULL PROOF OF THY MINISTRY".

The Lord Revealed to me that to have A Successful Ministry, A Pastor must seek to follow The Instructions of God in comparison to that of Free Will; The Lord Is Using Free Will to Manifest His Kingdom; therefore, Free Will must be used in The Church to recognize who it is that will do what God Command for His People to Do. Therefore, there must not be any forcing of individuals to do what is right, but a Freedom of Choice must be given to establish a person true intentions. By doing this, a lot of energy will be saved, because Truth must be Manifested.

All Glory, Honor and Praise goes to Our Eternal Father, Jesus Christ The Unlimited Mind of The Universe. From your Faithful Minister and Pastor Lerone Dinnall.

A Successful Ministry.

The Levels of Faith

Message # 29　　　　　　　　**Date Started March 12, 2016**
　　　　　　　　　　　　　　　　Date Finalized April 20, 2016.

GREETINGS FAMILY OF GOD, In The Name of Jesus Christ by which we are called to be a part of this Special; Blessed; and Holy Family. Called to speak on A Topic of this nature almost makes me feel nervous; thinking about the many different variables that this Topic carries; come to think about it, how much do I know about Faith, to actually think that I'm worthy to write A Message about not only Faith, but on The Levels of Faith. But then I realize that I was not the person that gave this Topic, instead it was God that Inspired and Gave this Topic, therefore, it is The Spirit of God that Will Inspired what will be said concerning this Topic; I'm just an Instrument willing to be Used by God.

I believe that before we can understand The Levels of Faith, we must first have an understanding of what Faith Is. According to The Bible in Hebrews Chapter 11:6.

"BUT WITHOUT FAITH IT IS IMPOSSIBLE TO PLEASE HIM: FOR HE THAT COMETH TO GOD MUST BELIEVE THAT HE IS,

AND THAT HE IS A REWARDER OF THEM THAT DILIGENTLY
SEEK HIM".

A Child of God that is seeking to exercise Faith in God, has got
to look at these words that says:

"MUST BELIEVE THAT HE IS".

The God that you're Serving Is The Only High God, and none
can compare to Him.

"AND THAT HE IS A REWARDER OF THEM THAT DILIGENTLY
SEEK HIM".

The God that you're Serving Will Come Through; Must Come
Through; Is Going to Come Through, even though your eyes may not
see the Evidence of how He Is Going to Come Through.

But this statement still does not answer what Is Faith; it more
shows a character of a person that has experience what it is like to be
living by Faith. In verse 1 of the same Chapter 11. This verse gave
a Clear definition of what Faith Is, by expressing to all those who
would read, to let us understand that Faith Starts with a word that is
Called NOW.

The word Now, which speaks of being present; coming into an
understanding of what is actually right and relevant; it speaks also
of existence of something happening which never happen before;
which many times take a while for many Child of God to reach that
particular time of Now; even though the World does not teach in this
manner, this is the way it actually is.

We have a whole lot to speak about Faith; therefore, we will
always be looking back at this word NOW, to better explain Faith
and The Levels of Faith.

According to Verse 1. Which Says:

"NOW FAITH IS THE SUBSTANCE OF THINGS HOPED FOR,
THE EVIDENCE OF THINGS NOT SEEN".

Now I've spent a long time looking on The Topic Faith, especially
when The Lord Inspired me to have Faith that I was going to start My
own business; I remembered when an incident took place concerning
My job at the company I was working at, that basically forced me
to fast track My plans to start my own business. I remember it like

135

it was yesterday; when every Message that came to my ears was to discourage me and to tell me all the negatives in life that I will be facing if I actually try to start a business of my own; this is what I remembered most in all that was being said:

"THE LORD CAME TO ME IN MY SLEEP AND TOLD ME THAT HE NEEDED ME TO DO A STUDY ON THE TOPIC FAITH"

I woke up the next morning believing in what I have heard, and started the Study of Faith; I remembered after one week of reading about Faith, I said to myself that I think I understood what the Topic is saying; then I went to my bed that same night, only to hear The Voice of The Lord Speaking to me again, that I must do a study on the Topic Faith. I went back to study the same materials concerning Faith, but I then realized that the understanding that I had before about the Topic got a lot deeper and more meaningful; therefore after two weeks I thought I had it; only to hear The Voice of The Lord came back to me in my sleep Telling me that I must do a study on the Topic Faith. This made me realize that there is always a deeper level to any Topic that you're researching concerning God. I did the study for a month, I did not hear The Voice of The Lord came back to Tell me that I must do a study about Faith; but that only made me realize that, what God Needed me to understand about Faith to carry me into My future for a new life to start My business, He Had Imparted The Knowledge that I need, to let me know that all things are possible with Him, if there is an evidence that it is being done by FAITH.

I tell you the truth, I find myself even now, doing more research on Faith and receiving more Revelations; therefore letting me know that there is always A Higher Level when it concerns God. To God be The Glory, it has passed 5 years, I'm doing my own Business and continuing to grow from strength to strength. Those who discouraged me are still where they are, wondering how and why has this happened.

Even though I did some research on this Topic before, I speak the truth; I'm in no way an expert concerning this Topic, because as I said before, that every time I have a look on this Topic, it gets a little deeper and deeper; therefore, even though I'm writing about this

Topic, I'm still open Minded to learn a lot more about this Topic than that which I thing I know. Nevertheless, I believe that My Experience in life along with My Study of this Topic will be able to help someone that is seeking to know more about God concerning Faith.

Let me share with you what God Has Explained to me concerning Faith and Verse 1 of Hebrews Chapter 11. The Lord Allowed me understand that for the action of Faith; when a believer actually comes to that particular time in their life that is called the NOW; this is to be compared to be A Visitation from God The Almighty Himself; that I don't care who you are, the moment you come in contact with your Now; you will realize that there is a difference, there must be a difference. Every Believer that is to Experience Faith will Experience A Supernatural Force that goes way ahead of everything that you ever learnt or ever will learn or ever believe, and will carry you to that which you need to now believe in; because Faith is always speaking of things that your own abilities will never be able to accomplish or even try to reach.

It is important to note that, if your Faith does not go in The Impossible, then it is not Faith; It stands only at a level of Hope, that you by yourself is able to fulfill. Many of us, we misunderstand what Faith really is; I hope this Message will help us to understand Faith a little more. The Lord Allowed for me to Realize that Faith the word that we look to use, it actually starts in The Mind of A Believer that is seeking to exercise that Faith.

Here is an explanation that The Lord Gave me:

FAITH: Molecules of thoughts coming together from the four directions of the Earth; East, West, North, and South; these thoughts cannot be seen, because they are Spiritual Inspirations or Messages that God Himself had Send to you; when they come together as an whole in your Mind, to Combine or to Form together, it now develops into Matter; something that you the individual can actually see as a picture in your thoughts; that allows you now to believe in the very impossible of that which you have seen, to confirm to you that it is actually possible.

All this is what takes place in the Mind; that remains in the Mind, until you the individual starts to put things in action according to the flesh to make sure that you reach the requirements of obtaining the actual promise of your Faith that you have seen.

I Ask My Readers to also consider this Revelation that God Has Allowed me to understand; and I promise you that the more you think about it, is the more you're going to realize that it is actually true. This is it:

"TIME IS THE MASTER OF FAITH; THEREFORE TIME IS THE ONLY OTHER ENEMY APART FROM DOUBT, WHICH PREVENTS FAITH FROM COMING INTO ACTION OF BEING FULFILLED".

"FAITH CONQUERS BOTH TIME AND DOUBT WHEN THE PERSON THAT IS EXERCISING FAITH; ALSO REALIZE THAT THERE IS A GREAT IMPORTANCE TO ALSO ENTERTAIN THE SPIRIT OF PATIENCE".

Not because something takes a long time to be fulfilled, that doesn't mean that through Faith in won't be fulfilled. However, Faith with the evidence of a Miracle is a Gift that conquers Time immediately; and this is one of the highest level your Faith could ever reach; but not everyone reaches this level of Faith over night, it takes time to get there.

Remember what I said, that, if that which you have Faith in is not Impossible and completely out of reach; then My Answer to that, is that it is not Faith, but only Hope. Therefore, because that which you have Faith in is so Great; the Process of Time has to take its course to enable that Faith to be Developed.

Have we ever considered within ourselves, that when God Gave us the Faith to believe in something that is going to happen; have we ever seen the time that should pass to allow that Faith to be fulfilled? _____.

I can say that many times the Answer is No.

Our job and responsibility is not to know when The Father Has Put in His Time to Fulfill that Faith that He Has Given to us; But our main job is to BELIEVE and to continue to feed that belief; to know that it is going to happen one day, not in our time; but in God's Time.

Therefore, We now understand that Faith Is Given and Revealed in portions; that has we go through one process of our life, then more will be Revealed; then before we know it, five or ten years of our lives has past, with that believer still on the walk of Faith, not Doubting, but Believing that were just a step closer to receive that Promise.

What I'm Revealing to My Readers is that, it's time for us to elevate from that which Stands at a Level of being just Hope, to move forward to that which is Faith. Although Hope has a significant element in that which is called Faith; Hope does not completely explain what Faith Is; or else it would not be called Faith, but will then remain at the word Hope.

Don't be confused; Hope is actually a Spirit that is a part of the Body that allows Faith to be what it is; but Hope by itself is not Faith, but only a part of the Built up. Confidence is also another Spirit in the Body of Faith, and also, and most important the Spirit that is called Focus. Let me say this, there is no way we can have Faith and not be a person that is actually brilliant in The Spirit to Be Focus.

Bishop Austin Whitfield Taught me something of great importance concerning Focus; this is what he said:

"WHEN YOU'RE TRULY FOCUSED; WHEN THERE IS A MESSAGE COMING TO YOU TO SOW A NEGATIVE SEED THAT WILL INTERRUPT YOUR FOCUS OR IN THIS CASE YOUR FAITH; YOUR FOCUS MUST BE SO STRONG AND DETERMINED THAT IT ACTUALLY FILTERS OUT ALL THE BAD SEEDS THAT ARE SPOKEN; THEREFORE NOT INTERRUPTING THE PATH OF YOUR FOCUS. BISHOP USUALLY REPEAT THESE WORDS: WHEN A PERSON SPEAKS TO HIM, REGARDING A BAD MESSAGE THAT THEY WOULD WANT HIM TO BELIEVE; HE WOULD SAY THAT HE DON'T HEAR WHAT THEY ARE SAYING, BUT HE ACTUALLY SEES WHAT THEY ARE SAYING"

This Example allows me to Understand that when someone speaks to me, I must always look on the end product of their Message to see whether The Message is giving life or the Message is seeking to destroy My Soul along with The Faith that I have Developed in God. Bishop would Say:

"NEGATIVE WORDS COMING FROM MESSAGES THAT PEOPLE

SPEAK, GOES THROUGH ONE EARS, AND COME DIRECTLY
THROUGH THE OTHER EARS; HE DOES NOT ALLOW IT TO ENTER
INTO HIS SOUL TO AFFECT HIS FOCUS OR HIS FAITH".

Looking back on what he Taught me, I can say Thank You God for Putting this Priest in My life. Allow me to bring forth A Revelation, we should always Give God Thanks for Putting an Inspiring Person in our lives; someone that Preached to us that we could become Saved; someone that Encourage us in this life of pain; someone that Helped us to keep on this path way of Faith.

Let's give an evidence of this Message of Faith coming from The Bible. Abraham, regarded has The Father of Faith; in Genesis Chapter 12, when Abraham's NOW came and Visited him, his entire life Changed. The Bible Said that God Spoke to Abraham and Told him what to do; and upon his Obedience, God Promised Abraham A Picture of what his life will now Become. Abraham did exactly what God Needed him to Do; thus chasing after that Picture of the life that God Has Promised him. According to Bible calculations, one of the main promise took 25 years to be fulfilled; but this didn't move Abraham, because he was sure that what God Had Promised, He Was Able to Perform.

Being The Father of Faith is a Title well deserved, because after waiting 25 years for the main promise of Divine Blessing Continuation, The Lord Then Asked him to Sacrifice that same promise; Abraham now being Seasoned with Faith realized that he was Serving The Mighty God, that made The Heavens and Earth, the Sea, the Land and all that is upon the land. Abraham Said within himself:

"I WILL DO WHAT GOD NEED ME TO DO, BECAUSE EVEN THOUGH THIS IS MY PROMISE CHILD, THE GOD THAT I SERVE IS MORE THAN ABLE TO RESURRECT THIS CHILD FROM DEATH; SEEING THAT THIS CHILD CAME FROM A WOMB THAT WAS DEAD".

Studying about Faith, I've gotten to realize that there is a lot that needs to be said about Faith to let us understand the Process a lot better. Here is a Big Question that must be Asked:

Do you think that everyone has Faith? _____.

The Answer I would give to that Question is Yes.

But then I can just imagine some of My Readers now saying that they don't think that's true.

But studying about Faith made me realize that Faith is A Spirit that is open to all Mankind, especially those who are Serving God.

Let's look on it this way; Do all Human Being have a Brain? _____.

The Answer is Yes; But in a twist, can we agree that not every Human Being use their Brain to their full Potential. This however does not stop us from having the capacity to use that Brain, but many of us have not Received of The Release from God for Access to be granted that our Minds will be set Free. But there still remains the great Potential for our Minds to be Awaken only if we Turn to God.

PROVE FOR THOSE WHO ARE NOT SAVED

Many of us before we got Saved; believed that Christ Could Make A Difference in our lives, especially when we discover what God Has Done in someone life that we know about. It was that little evidence of Faith that caused us to turn around to now become A Child of God. Being a Sinner, living a life far away from God; if there wasn't Faith involved we would have never changed our lifestyle to believe that there is a better life in God. Jesus Christ Said to the woman with the issue of blood that Touched Him:

"YOUR FAITH HAS MADE YOU WHOLE"

There was a woman in The Book of St Luke Chapter 7:36-50. This is the story in summary: This woman came into an house where Jesus Christ was a Guest, she being a well-known sinner, exercised her Faith, brought forth an Alabaster box of precious Ointment; stood at the Feet of Jesus Christ weeping because she knew that she was undeserved of even being in the same place with the Man that came from God. She took of the Ointment, and Anointed The Feet of Jesus Christ; The Bible Said that she took her own hair that is on her head, to wipe The Feet of Jesus Christ. The Bible Said that the Pharisee that

Invited Jesus Christ to his home saw it, and immediately started to judge; because those that were in the house knew the woman, and her lifestyle. He said within himself, this man can't be a Prophet, because if He was; He should have known the type of woman that is touching Him. The Bible Said that Jesus Knew what he was thinking; and Responded to him; letting him know that a person who have received at lot more pardon, will be a lot more appreciative of everything that God Has Done for them. The Lord Said unto the woman that was a sinner:

"THY SINS ARE FORGIVEN".

He also Said to the woman who was a sinner:

"THY FAITH HATH SAVED THEE; GO IN PEACE".

This Scripture Gives evidence to us, to let us know that, both Sinner and Children of God, does possess Faith. The Centurion whose servant was sick unto death, said to Jesus Christ; Lord, Speak The Word and my servant shall be healed; Jesus Christ Said to him:

"I HAVE NOT FOUND SO GREAT FAITH, NO NOT IN ISRAEL; AND BECAUSE OF THAT FAITH THAT HE HAD SEEN, NOT NECESSARILY COMING FROM A PERSON WHO IS AN ISRAELITE; ALLOWED HIM TO DECLARE THAT MANY SHALL COME FROM THE EAST, WEST, NORTH AND SOUTH AND SIT DOWN WITH ABRAHAM; ISAAC AND JACOB IN THE KINGDOM OF HEAVEN; AND THOSE WHO THE KINGDOM IS MADE FOR; BECAUSE OF THE LACK OF FAITH WILL BE CAST INTO OUTER DARKNESS".

It is a good thing; that studying this Topic make us realize that all of us as human beings has a level of Faith inside of us; It is a bad thing, to know that not all of us is using this Faith to Evolve in God. Has it stands, that all have Faith; just as how all breed the breath of life that is given to us; and also it is known that all have some type of Talent, but not everyone uses that Talent. It must also be noted that not all of us is at the same level of Faith as the other. Whether you want to believe it or not, it is true; Faith actually Grows and become Greater and even Greater than that we could ever image.

The Bible Has Proven that many times, sinners possess more Faith than that of A Child of God. I wander to myself why is that?

The answer that I came up with is that; Sinners have nothing to lose; because they have already tried every other method; and it did not work. Therefore giving God a try now; they give it their all. For Christian, this is My belief; because we have already given our lives to God; we believe that everything must automatically fall in place, with the evidence of no actions. In other words, what I'm saying is that many of us are just too Lazy.

The Bible Declares to us, that the children of men are wiser than The Children of God. Reason for this is because The Children of God are not Discipline; therefore, we fall in a spirit that we just settle for whatever comes our way. My People Are Destroyed for A LACK OF KNOWLEDGE. We don't seek to know more about God, therefore we are lagging behind.

EXAMPLES FOR CHRISTIANS

Jesus Christ Said, If you have Faith as a grain of Mustard seed, you shall say to this mountain be removed and be cast in the midst of the sea. This He Spoke to them after He Cursed the Fig tree, and the next morning they saw that His Words came to past; being amazed that He Just Spoke and it Happened.

Jesus Christ after Imparting on His Twelve Disciple Power to cast out Demons and to perform miracles; there came a man with his son, possessed with Demons; brought him to His Disciple, that they should Pray for his son to be delivered from the afflictions of the Devil; when they Prayed; they found out that the work was not done, they came up short. The man then brought his son to Jesus Christ, of which He Said; Oh ye of little Faith; speaking to His Disciples; when they Asked Him; why could not we cast the Demon out; He Continue by Telling them; Howbeit these kinds goeth not out but by Fasting and Prayer. This He Said to Demonstrate to His Disciples and to us that a person may have Faith; but to Perform Greater Works; it demands that such a person seek for Greater Faith, which does exist.

This explanation brings forth a point to a Fact that I was always making, but not a lot of people cares to listen. I always said that not everyone should be called to Lay Hands; Note, everyone can lay hands on someone if they feel like doing so; but that does not mean that A Miracle or Healing or Deliverance will take place; that does not mean that when they have actually finished Praying; The Approval that only God Can Send, actually took place because He Heard that Prayer. I said to all My Members of The Church:

"AFTER GIVING GOD ALL THE SERVICE AND SACRIFICE THAT IS TO BE OFFERED; WHEN WE NOW GO TO HIM IN PRAYER; THIS IS THE BIG QUESTION:

DID GOD HEAR"?

WAS THE SERVICE AND SACRIFICE ACCEPTABLE THAT YOU FORCED GOD NOT ONLY TO HEAR, BUT ALSO TO GRANT HIS FAVOURS UPON YOUR REQUEST?"

Only those who have reached a Level of Faith to do whatever work that is desired, will be the ones that will be able to perform such a Miracle or Healing. The Lord Would let us know before leaving this earth, that Greater Works than that which He Has Done, shall we be also able to Perform. But these Greater Works Children of God, must require A Greater Level of Faith; if there is No Greater Faith; No Greater Relationship with God; No Greater Fasting; No Greater Prayer; No Greater Revelations; there will be No Greater Works.

I have seen with my own eyes many of God's People trying to lay hands on other people for Deliverance; these are Saints that don't have a strong Prayer life; these are Saints that say that they cannot afford to Fast; or can't find no time to Fast. Then, let me ask this Question:

How in God's Name will that person ever be able to Declare and Decree God's Miracle on someone life? _____.

CANNOT WORK!

If you don't believe me you can try it for yourself; but don't say I didn't warn you!

It was Brother Paul when he was Preaching and doing Miracles in Ephesus, and also casting out demons; there were seven sons of Sceva, a man who was a Priest and also a Jew; his sons saw what

Paul was doing through The Mighty Power of God; they took it upon themselves to go forth to do the same thing that Paul was doing, maybe saying to themselves that they are the sons of the Priest; and if this man Paul is able to do these Miracle, then we should also be able to do it. Thinking that if they but just call on The Name of Jesus Christ, that they heard Paul called upon, then they too will be able to perform the Miracles that they saw Paul did.

THE BIBLE SAID THAT THE EVIL SPIRIT ANSWERED AND SAID TO THEM; JESUS I KNOW; PAUL I KNOW; BUT WHO ARE YE!

The Bible Said that the evil spirit used the man in which he was in, to beat these men and wound them that they ran out of the house naked. Act Chapter 19:8-20. The evil spirit recognize that there was NO WEIGHT; a lot of talking and NO SUBSTANCE of The Living Spirit of God in these men. This made me realize what God Told me a while back, when I was not Praying as how I should be Praying; The Lord Said:

"MY SON, THE DEVIL IS NOT AFRAID OF YOU; THE DEVIL IS AFRAID OF GOD; THEREFORE, YOU MUST PRAY MORE OFTEN, SO THAT I CAN PROTECT YOU FROM THE PLANS OF THE DEVIL".

These sons of Sceva, could not understand the Weight; the Power; the Authority; the Level of Faith that was in Paul; that came through a lot of Fasting and Prayers; Sufferings and Pain; Persecutions and Hardship, Shipwrecks and Beatings; that enabled him to be the man with that type of Faith and Anointing to cast out demons and do Great Works. So should we all recognize, that A Greater Level of Faith is going to come with Greater Level of Discipline, to know what God Requires.

There is something that is of great importance that we all must know; Faith differs, according to the individual; meaning that My Faith can never be your Faith; neither can your Faith Be My Faith. Your Faith is your NOW; it is like your shoe size; or to make it seem more difficult; it's like your D.N.A. No matter how long and hard someone tries to live your life; it just will not fit; they will one day be weary of pretending. Now you will understand that many times when God Brings your NOW in the figure of your Mind; you should allow it to stay there and work on it through process. Because even if you happen to tell someone about the Revelation of your NOW; they will not understand it; they will even Envy and Malice you, because they will realize that your NOW; your Revelation of Faith is far superior to what they could ever imagine.

Take a look on the Story of Joseph; his NOW was Revealed to him and through his excitement, he taught that because he and his family grew up in the same house it would automatically mean that they must love him. Has it was Established, when Joseph revealed his NOW; his brethren grew to hate him even more, because they could not imagine nor conceive it in their heart to think that such a thing is even possible; his own father rebuked him; being also a man of Faith. We know the story, they plan to kill him, because there was no way they wanted to even see any evidence of him their younger brother being ruler over them. If it had not been for God on his side; they might have had their way. There is something about your NOW; it means that GOD The Almighty Is In It; and no matter what the enemy does, as long as you are persistent to walk in the Faith of your NOW, God Will be more than ABLE to Fulfill it.

I would like to give My Testimony; I grew up going to School, hearing almost everyone in School; out of School, telling me that I am not going to become anything. In Primary School, to part of High School, I could not move out of the lowest class, no matter what I did. I would often be asked to call My Parents that the Teacher and Principal talk to them concerning My progress; and this was always the Statement:

"HE CAN LEARN, HE JUST NEED SOMEONE TO PUSH HIM".

With that being said, the Principal decided to put me in the upper class, for this to be a tool to help push me. This was one of the most embarrassing time in My life; for the first two weeks in the upper class, what the Teacher did mostly was Spelling; My Education level for spelling was about 25% or 30% at that time. I got teased and humiliated every day; because I spelled the lease amount of words. It got worse when I decided to copy off one of My Class mate book work; My Class mate was a girl; I copied even her name and gave it to the Teacher; the Teacher embarrassed me that day before the whole class; the next day I went right back to the lower class and never went back to the upper class even though the teacher came for me.

You may be asking, why am I sharing this with My Readers? The Answer Is; I want to help someone who may be going through a time in their life that they may think that there is no tomorrow. To complete My Testimony; I started believing that I would come out to be nothing.

Can someone say BUT GOD!

Saints I speak the truth; My NOW Came; and God Began to Tell me the opposite of what everyone else was telling me; He Installed in My Life A Great Level of Faith; and Allowed me to Understand that He Is Able. The first thing The Lord Did was to Change My Location, "SEPARATION"; because we all need to know by now, that if God Is Going to Work in our lives, the Environment has to change.

There must be a Letting go of the OLD in order for THE NEW to take over. THE PAST must be the past in order for THE FUTURE to be realized.

To let My Readers understand what God Did in summary; The moment I moved from one parish to another; I was introduce to Church; I got Baptized; a new location also meant that there is a new school; the Principal of the new school was influence to try with me in the upper class; Saints, I stayed in the upper class; I did evening classes; I learned how to read and spell by breaking up words into syllables; I got deputy prefect; I leaved high school in the upper class; I got the highest marks in exam for My Training program; and when I went back to school to pick up My Results; the Principal offered me a job to Teach My Skill area and also to go to Teachers College; I decline that opportunity, because that wasn't My Passion.

GOD IS GOOD.

Many people may ask why I shared this Testimony; I will say, I want to help someone that is struggling to believe; wondering whether or not if God Can Do It. My God Specializes in all things that are Impossible. My past can no longer hurt me; neither am I ashamed anymore. It is not your beginning; it's your ending; with

God it's not your past, it's your future; it's not how people look on you or judge you; it's how God Looks on you; remember that!

I often tell many people that are seeking to give their lives over to God, and is struggling to make up their Mind; I told them that it is the best decision. To many of My friends who have not yet Given over to God's Will; God Is Saying I LOVE YOU, God Never Looks on what you are right now, because He Can't Look on Sin; God Looks on you and Loves you because of the Saint of God He Is Able to Make you. Many people have the excuse of saying BUT; BUT; BUT. God Is Saying I CAN; I CAN; I CAN; I CAN Forget about your past, and bring you into a Future that you will never believe.

Back to Faith; a minimum of two or three persons can reach a level of Faith that cause great things to happen. But the verb in that sentence is that all parties have reach that level, to allow that which you seek for from God to actually Happen. You may find this happening a lot when you go to Church in the assemble where God's People are; If your Praying, or The Church is Praying over a particular request; but for some reason, there is just not the Connection you desire; nor do you feel that you have Touch God for Him to Move that Mountain to Allow the request to be Answered. You know within yourself that you have Faith that it can come through; but what you're not realizing is that you may be amongst MIX MULTITUDES. Your surroundings do affect your progress has it was proven in my Testimony. Not because you're in Church, that doesn't mean that your Prayers cannot be Blocked.

We must always remember that The Church is built upon the gates of hell. And if it is that there is not someone in The Church to marshal the assembly to Serve God in the right manner; giving of The Accepted Sacrifice; then I'm afraid that you will be Praying for a long time, without receiving an answer. If two or three are gathered together in My Name to Seek My Face; there am I in the midst of them to Hear and to Answer their Prayer.

Many times when we need a breakthrough for a Faith to come to past; we have got to find the courage to move away from the noise; to seek two more persons that is of the same level of Faith that we have; start a Prayer Meeting; and then we will get to realize that there was nothing wrong with our level of Faith, it's just that we never had someone to share that level of Faith with that the connection will be made. Then and only then will we realize that God Is Not Always in the Noise, or in the crowd; but in the whisper of two and three that are True Worshippers; that is of the same level of Faith; which can move ANY MOUNTAIN.

Many times we will find in Churches persons who are Pillars of Unrighteousness, that have cemented their position in The Church; and it is these persons that are put in responsibilities to bring the members of The Church into Worship or Prayer before God. Now you will see why there is a struggle at times to even Worship; because the Worship is not Accepted. There is a struggle to feel that your Prayer is Answered; because although you Prayed, and your living the best life that you can live being A Child of God; and you have the Faith; the Question still remains; after you have done that; DID GOD HEAR YOUR PRAYER? _____.

We all need to know that there is a decease that is called Sin, which God Has to Keep Away from, or else those who have the sin will die if God Shows up; and there is no way God and Sin will ever mix. Therefore, if we have Sin in our members that is unforgiven, or it is that we are around Sin; this will greatly affect our chances of God Hearing our Prayers.

Take for Example Cain, when he offered his Sacrifice to God; The Bible Said that God Had No Respect unto Cain's Sacrifice. The four hundred prophets that Elijah asked to call upon their god; though they were calling from morning to evening; because they knew not The True and Living God; there was no answer. It is safe to say that, anyone who is offering a Sacrifice unworthy; then that Sacrifice will not be Accepted; even if that person is representing a whole lot of people. Support doesn't Shake God; it is a broken and a contrite heart; that's what God Recognize.

You may hear many people come to you and say this to you concerning your Faith, when they actually see that it has come through; this is what I hear many people saying:

149

"IT CAME TO ME ALSO TO DO SOMETHING OF THE SAME EFFORT THAT YOU HAVE ACCOMPLISH; I ALWAYS WANTED TO DO SOMETHING LIKE THAT; BUT THE TIME HAS NOT YET COME; OR I COULD NOT BE BOTHERED, OR I JUST DID NOT HAVE THE TIME TO PURSUE A CHALLENGE OF THAT TYPE; THEREFORE, I DECIDED NOT TO GO AFTER THAT SPARK OF FAITH".

I know that those that are living by Faith, have heard something like that. It is not yet Faith until it has been, or is being pursued by you. One Major Factor that comes up beside our Faith is a word and spirit that is called FEAR; which brings forth DOUBT. If you're moving by Faith; you have got to overcome Fear. If you can't overcome Fear; then you can't pursue after Faith. No Movement; No Action; which means No Victory. It can be said that those that have Faith is one Channel; or one Focused; not easily distracted, and not easily changed.

I would like to share this with My Readers concerning Faith: Faith the being has A Foundation in the lives of those who walk in The Spirit of Faith. Foundation meaning that a desire to have Faith in someone or something comes from the basic instruction of a Parent or Pastor to Teach and to Train their child in the belief that there is A God, Who Can and Will do Wonders for those who Trust in Him.

If there is a Study done to identify the success of people with Great Faith, the results will Manifest that these People, all of them had A Foundation that their parents taught them well to Fear and to Trust The Almighty GOD; their parents brought them up in Church and most importantly Sunday or Saturday School.

There is a Story in The Bible that best describe this event; In The Book of Daniel Chapter 3. The Bible explain that king Nebuchadnezzar made an image of gold, and gave a command that all should bow down and worship the image that he had set up. When it was told the king that three men which he had set up to rule and govern, refused to bow down and worship his image; the king was now furious; and desired to now put these men to death. After giving them one final warning of what he was going to do, if they did not bow down and worship the image; The three young men answered the king and told him that:

"WE ARE NOT CAREFUL TO ANSWER YOU IN THIS MATTER;
IF IT BE SO, OUR GOD WHOM WE SERVE IS ABLE TO DELIVER
US FROM THE BURNING FIERY FURNACE, AND HE WILL
DELIVER US OUT OF THINE HAND, O KING".

So said; so it was done. The king asked his Counsellors:

"DID NOT WE CAST THREE MEN BOUND INTO THE MIDST OF
THE FIRE? THEY SAID TRUE O KING. THE KING REPLIED; LO, I
SEE FOUR MEN LOOSE, WALKING IN THE MIDST OF THE FIRE,
AND THEY HAVE NO HURT; AND THE FORM OF THE FOURTH IS
LIKE THE SON OF GOD".

Nebuchadnezzar witness first hand, the Faith that these young men possessed; because they were but just youths when they came into Babylon with Daniel. But there was a FOUNDATION in the lives of these young men; that not even the words of a king and the evidence of fire burning above it natural limits; not even death itself could have shaken the Foundation of the Faith that these men had in The True and Living God. Many of us reading this Message, may have a child; Question to you:

➤ HAVE YOU STARTED THE FOUNDATION OF FAITH IN THE
   LIFE OF YOUR OWN CHILD?

   _____.

➤ ARE YOU SPENDING ENOUGH TIME TO LET THEM KNOW
   THAT THERE IS A TRUE AND LIVING GOD?

   _____.

➤ DO YOU LET THEM KNOW THAT GOD CAN WALK WITH
   THEM AND HE CAN TALK WITH THEM?

   _____.

➤ HAVE YOU CEMENTED IN THEM TO KNOW THAT GOD IS
   TO BE PRAISED AND WORSHIP AT ALL TIMES?

   _____.

This is the Foundation that the three Hebrew boys had; no one could fool them about their God; because they knew Him in a Personal way. After the king saw that Great Miracle; the king made a Decree, that every People, Nation, and Language, which speak anything amiss against The God of Shadrach; Meshach; and Abed-nego; shall be cut in pieces, and their house shall be made a dunghill: Because there is no other God that Can Deliver after this sort.

QUESTION: Will we have Faith like this; to bring Honour to Our True and Living God. If we are not attempting to reach a level of Faith like this; then it doesn't make sense we talk about Faith.

Light Bulb People of God!

FAITH IS HARD WORK!

A lazy man cannot exercise Faith; because Faith means Movement. And because Faith's Spirit is recognize by the Movement of an Individual, it is tied into agreement with The First Manifestation of The Spirit of God which is to MOVE, therefore a person with The Spirit of Faith is automatically Pleasing God because of adopting of The Wave of The Spirit of God. A person that knows nothing about Prayer and Fasting; they can never know the true value of Faith; will never see the true power that comes from Faith; because they have not yet graduated to the next level of Faith. One of the most important Ingredient of Faith is YOU, the believer of that Faith, the Vessel which stores that type of Faith; you are the person that will physical Show; Manifest and Prove to others that God Can Indeed Do that which you desire for God to Do, which is completely in God's Will; because My Testimony is to let you know that God Did It for me.

It's the person that is experiencing their NOW FAITH, will be able to show to others how Big their God Truly Is; it is your life that will draw others to come, having the same desire to Serve God with all their Hearts, Mind and Soul. It is your Faith that is going to make you an example before all those who see you.

The last thing that I would like to share with My Readers about this Topic, is a Story in The Book of Ruth. The Bible would let us know that Naomi's Husband and both her sons died. After such Testing times, Naomi decided to go back to her place of birth; She had still two of her daughter in law, that were wives to her sons; who decided that they were going to follow after their Mother in law. This action clearly demonstrated that Naomi was a good Mother in law. After great persuasion; one of her daughter in law decided to go back to her father's house; but Ruth, the other daughter in law was Persistent; Determined; can I also say that she was Stubborn in her will; not to leave her mother in law, no matter what she said or did.

The Bible Said that Naomi, when she saw that Ruth was "STEADFASTLY MINDED" to go with her, then she left speaking unto her.

I brought up this Story, because I Need My Readers to see exactly what is necessary for us to fulfill our Faith in God. If your Faith have not reached a point in your life that you're completely STEADFASTLY MINDED; then you don't know what it even takes to begin this journey of Faith. Your Faith must be so REAL, that you completely don't care what other people are saying about the walk that you're on. You don't even care if that which you have Faith in cost you your life; because that's what Faith is. It comes from The Spiritual; Manifest itself in the Physical; in order to go right back to The Spiritual.

Your Faith can only be fulfilled when you have reached the time and the place for it to be fulfilled; that's when GOD'S DECLARE meets with GOD'S DECREED. When you have reach that place; God Will Now Say: YES, I AM GOD that Gives this Faith Life; and I AM GOD that Is Going to Fulfill that which I Say I Am Going To Do in your life.

I Hope that you have enjoyed this Message; I know that it's more than what you are accustom to be Reading; but believe me when I tell you that, I never knew that it was going to be so long. And come to think about it; this Message is not even finished; because has you have realized by now; God's Understanding keeps on growing and growing in our Minds.

There is a lot more about Faith that needs to be discovered; we've only but just scratch the surface. Because it's just only a piece of His knowledge is known. Therefore, we can basically say that this is only Level one, of The Levels of Faith.

May God Continue to Bless you; Keep you. Let us all grow together in this type of Faith. Let us Praise The Lord of lords and The King of all kings, Jesus Christ. From the Servant of God; Your Brother; Your Friend; Your Minister and Pastor Lerone Dinnall.

CLIMB THROUGH THE LEVELS OF FAITH.

Write your Personal Revelation from God, add your Special Touch to your Book from this Ministry.

1. _____
2. _____
3. _____
4. _____
5. _____
6. _____
7. _____
8. _____
9. _____
10. _____
11. _____
12. _____
13. _____
14. _____
15. _____
16. _____
17. _____
18. _____
19. _____
20. _____
21. _____
22. _____
23. _____
24. _____
25. _____

CLOSING SCRIPTURE

REVELATION CHAPTER 22:1-17.

"And he shew me a pure river of water of life, clear as crystal, proceeding out of The Throne of God and of The Lamb. In the midst of the street of it, and on either side of the river, was there the tree of life, which bare twelve manner of fruits, and yielded her fruit every month: and the leaves of the tree were for the healing of the nations. And there shall be no more curse: but The Throne of God and of The Lamb shall be in it; and His Servants shall Serve Him: And they shall see His Face; and His Name shall be in their foreheads. And there shall be no night there; and they need no candle, neither light from the sun; for The Lord God Giveth them light: and they shall reign for ever and ever.

And he said unto me, these sayings are Faithful and True: and The Lord God of The Holy Prophets sent His Angel to shew unto His Servants the things which must shortly be done. Behold I Come Quickly: Blessed is he that keepeth the sayings of the prophesy of this Book. And I John saw these things, and heard them. And when I had heard and seen, I fell down to worship before the feet of the Angel which shewed me these things. Then said he unto me, See thou do it not: for I am thy fellowservant, and of thy brethren the prophets, and of them which keep the sayings of this Book: Worship God. And he said unto me, Seal not the sayings of the prophesy of this Book: for the time is at hand. He that is unjust, let him be unjust still: and he which is filthy, let him be filthy still: and he that is righteous, let him be righteous still: and he that is holy, let him be holy still.

And, Behold, I Come Quickly; and My Reward is with Me, to Give every man according as his work shall be. I Am Alpha and Omega, The Beginning and The End, The First and The Last. Blessed are they that do His Commandments, that they may have right to the Tree of Life, and may enter in through the Gates into the City. For without are dogs, and sorcerers, and whoremongers, and murderers, and idolaters, and whosoever loveth and maketh a lie. I Jesus have Sent Mine Angel to Testify unto you these things in The Churches. I Am The Root and Offspring of David, and The Bright and Morning Star. And The Spirit and The Bride Say, Come. And let him that heareth say, Come. And let him that is athrist come. And whosoever will, let him take the water of life freely".

CONCLUSION

THE LORD INSTRUCTED ME to use the closing Scripture of this Book, to thus remind His People of The Great Rewards that is awaiting His People that have Chosen to take the right road in life that will lead to the Straight and Narrow way, and will no doubt lead to Eternal Rest with The Father Above.

It is the final Chapter of life, it is now the Season that The Lord Will Open the eyes of many to see that the devil's plan and way of life will only end in destruction. The Lord Has Released An Anointing through these Books and also in the World for those who are to be Saved, they must now PUSH, FORCE, and FIGHT to plant themselves in The Vineyard of God, because the Harvest is plenty, there is a lot of Souls still to be set Free, but the laborers are Few. I speak by The Spirit of God, The Lord Said:

"IT IS NOW THE ELEVENTH HOUR, IT'S TIME FOR EVERYONE TO MAKE THEIR CALLING AN ELECTION SURE, TO THUS RECEIVE THEIR DUE REWARD".

The release of this Book follows the usual Burning that The Lord Always Provides when He Needs me to do something for the benefit of The Kingdom of Heaven. Therefore, I am Positive that whoever comes in contact with even one version of these Messages, I know that The Divine Intelligence that taught me how to be An Author and A Pastor, will also confirm within your Souls to Identify that this is not a man that is speaking, but rather it is The Spirit of God within A Vessel that Speaks; and The Lord Is Saying:

"It is Time for The Tithes of the land to Draw Closer to Him before it is too late".

Let All Glory Be Offered to The King of kings, and The Lord of all lords, Jesus Christ The Lamb of God. At The Name of Jesus Christ Every Knee Must Bow, and all Tongues will confess that Jesus Christ Is Lord.

From The Ministry of The Church of Jesus Christ Fellowship Savannah Cross Limited Jamaica West Indies. Look forward to the next Book that will be released when The Lord Provides His Burning. God Bless.